THE SPEECH

THE
SPEECH

*On Corporate Greed and the
Decline of Our Middle Class*

Senator Bernie Sanders

NATION
BOOKS
New York

Introduction Copyright © 2015 by Senator Bernie Sanders
Published by Nation Books, A Member of the Perseus Books Group
116 East 16th Street, 8th Floor
New York, NY 10003

Nation Books is a co-publishing venture of the Nation Institute and the Perseus Books Group

Books published by Nation Books are available at special discounts for bulk purchases in the United States by corporations, institutions, and other organizations. For more information, please contact the Special Markets Department at the Perseus Books Group, 2300 Chestnut Street, Suite 200, Philadelphia, PA 19103, or call (800) 810-4145, ext. 5000, or e-mail special .markets@perseusbooks.com.

A CIP catalog record for this book is available from the Library of Congress.
LCCN 2011920256
ISBN: 978-1-56858-684-7 (2011 paperback)
ISBN: 978-1-56858-685-4 (2011 e-book)
ISBN: 978-1-56858-553-6 (2015 paperback)
ISBN: 978-1-56858-554-3 (2015 e-book)

10 9 8 7 6 5 4 3 2 1

This book is dedicated to my four wonderful children,
Levi, Heather, Carina, and Dave,
and my wonderful grandchildren,
Sunnee, Cole, Ryleigh, Grayson, Ella Jane, and Tess.
May they live long and happy lives in a nation
full of hope, opportunity, prosperity, and security.

Acknowledgments

No United States Senator accomplishes much without a great staff. And I have one of the best. I want to thank all of those staff members, current and in the past, for the help they have provided me in formulating the ideas that appear in this book.

It is seldom that the men and women who work on the floor of the Senate to transcribe what is said and then type their stenographic notes into the text that becomes the official *Congressional Record* are recognized for their labors. I wish to recognize them here, and to add that the text of my speech contained in this book differs from the *Congressional Record* only in that some minor factual errors made during the course of my eight-hour speech have been silently corrected, and a half-dozen transitional words have been added to link sentences that made sense orally but not in the written version.

Proceeds

All authorial proceeds of this book will go to charitable, non-profit organizations in the State of Vermont—mostly relating to the needs of children.

Introduction to the 2015 Edition

When I formally announced my candidacy for president in my hometown of Burlington, Vermont, more than 5,000 people showed up to cheer us on. Within weeks, we had 10,000 people in Madison, Wisconsin. Then there were 15,000 in Seattle, 28,000 in Portland, 27,000 in Los Angeles. As the summer of 2015 wore on, we attracted the largest crowds of any campaign in the first caucus state of Iowa and the first primary state of New Hampshire.

People are coming out because the very, very rich are getting richer, while the rest of us are getting poorer—they feel the rigged economy every day. They feel it when they open up their bills around the kitchen table, pull items out of their grocery carts, or tell their kids their jackets can last one more winter.

Traveling around the country, I keep hearing the same thing: Americans are fed up with the way things are going. They're sick of cuts to social services, and threats to vital programs like Social Security, while their hard-earned tax dollars are pilfered to pay for unnecessary wars and corporate welfare. They're sick of working longer hours for lower wages just to line the pockets of the rich—who, in turn, are outsourcing their jobs through bad trade deals and undercutting our ability to bargain for fair wages. And they're sick of corporate greed destroying our political system, as Big Money interests spend unlimited sums of money to elect the candidates of their choice.

In the last two years, 15 people saw a $170 billion increase in their wealth, while 45 million Americans live in poverty. That in my view is not justice. That is a rigged economy, designed by the wealthiest people in this country to benefit the wealthiest people in this country at the expense of everybody else.

And hundreds of thousands of Americans are standing up and demanding change.

What I believe from the bottom of my heart is that I cannot do it alone.

No president can take on Wall Street, corporate America, the corporate media, the Koch brothers, all the Big Money interests, unless there's a mobilized force of millions and millions of people who stand together and demand government work for all of us, not just the wealthiest people in this country.

We've done this by putting people at the center of our campaign—without a Super PAC funded by billionaires, bankers, or Big Business. Our movement doesn't represent their interests and we don't want their money. Instead, we have relied on small contributions from working people.

When we started this campaign, I knew we had a message that would resonate with the American people.

It isn't the first time. There was a similar reaction when I gave a long speech on the Senate floor five years ago.

On Friday, December 10, 2010, I woke up at my usual time, had my usual breakfast of oatmeal and coffee at the Dirksen Senate Building, and then had a typical daily discussion with some of my staff. At 10:30 a.m., I walked onto the floor of the Senate and began a speech. It went on for eight and a half hours—until 7 p.m.

I had promised to do everything I could to oppose what I believed was a very bad tax agreement pushed by Republicans. At a time when this country had a $14.8 trillion dollar national debt and the most unequal distribution of wealth and income of any major country, it seemed to me totally absurd to provide hundreds of billions in tax breaks for millionaires and billionaires.

I decided to object in the loudest way I knew, by mounting what some referred to as a filibuster but what was, in reality, a long speech on a very important subject. I did not want merely to speak about the agreement, nor even about the politics of compromise and concession. I tried my best to state what I thought to be the essential fact of our times: that the concentration of wealth and power in the hands of a few families, at a time when tens of millions of Americans struggle to get by and tens of millions more Americans are watching the underpinnings of their middle-class lives take repeated hits, is turning our country into a plutocracy.

What does it say about our economy and the political choices we make about it on Capitol Hill that, today, despite all the huge increases in productivity and technology that we've seen in recent decades, a two-income family now has less disposable income than a one-income family did thirty years ago? Why is it that Americans work the longest hours of any people in the industrialized world?

What is the correlation between the United States having, by far, the highest rate of childhood poverty of any major country while we also have more people in jail? Doesn't it make more sense to invest in our kids than in jail construction?

How does it reflect upon our political and legal system when the crooks on Wall Street who caused the horrendous recession now earn more money than they did before their banks were bailed out by the taxpayers? How come none of them are in jail? And what does it mean when three out of the top four "too big to fail" banks in this country are now larger than they were before the Wall Street collapse, with assets of over half the GDP of the country?

What does it mean to the economic future of our country that we're losing factories and millions of good-paying jobs, and that it is harder and harder to buy products manu-factured in America? How does it happen that CEOs of large corporations boast about the advantages of outsourcing their production and jobs to China, but when hard times hit, they come running to U.S. taxpayers for a bailout?

And on, and on, and on!

What does it feel like to stand and talk for eight hours when you can't leave the floor, eat, or go to the bathroom—and know that a TV camera is on you all that time? It's hard. The aftereffect hit me a few days later when I found myself *very, very* tired. During the speech itself, my legs began to cramp up a bit. My voice also became very hoarse.

When I walked onto the floor, I had no idea how long I would stay there. When I was mayor of Burlington, Ver-mont, in the 1980s, I sometimes gave speeches for as long as an hour. That was it. Would I last three hours, five hours, twenty hours? I really didn't know. What I was clear about in my own mind, however, was that I wasn't going to read from the phone book or sing songs just to eat up time. I wanted to speak for as long as I had something relevant to say. While I didn't have a prepared script for the speech, I mostly worked off of previous speeches I had given or articles that I had written and occasionally excerpts from some books I had read. I would read a few lines or pages and go off from there. Twice, colleagues came to the floor and engaged in what we call a colloquy. I remain grateful to senators Sherrod Brown and Mary Landrieu for their support of my effort.

Let me also warn the good readers of this book that it contains some repetition. This is not an accident. In giving this speech I was more than aware that most people were not going to be listening to it in its entirety. I suspected that most people would tune in for half an hour or an hour and then move on with their lives. I made it a point to keep returning to my basic themes.

Was I surprised about the kind of attention that the speech received? Are you kidding? The phones in both my Washington and Vermont offices never stopped ringing. In Vermont, every one of my eight staff people did nothing else all day but respond to calls—thousands of calls. And e-mails! The Senate servers crashed because of the huge number of people who wanted to watch the speech live online, apparently C-SPAN 2 had an exceptional day. According to the *New York Times*, my speech was the most tweeted event in the world on that day. There were front-page stories in newspapers around the country and the speech was covered widely in the international media. The number of people who friended me on Facebook doubled the previous total in one day, and visits to my website went sky-high. Some journalists even claimed that Obama held an unscheduled, impromptu press conference with former president Bill Clinton, who defended the tax deal, in order to divert media attention away from what I was doing on the Senate floor.

Despite my best efforts and the hard work of many other members of Congress, we lost the vote and a very bad agreement was signed into law.

Was my eight-and-a-half-hour speech worth the effort? Absolutely! If this country is going to move forward in a new direction, if we're going to save the middle class and change our national priorities, we have got to cut through the obfuscating fog created by the corporate mainstream media and start focusing on the life-and-death issues that working families really care about.

The very strong response to my speech in 2010 and our campaign tells me that the hunger for a discussion about economic truths, for a counterattack on the ferocious assaults that are taking place against working families, and for a practical plan on how we can reverse the obscene politics that favor the rich over the middle class and disadvantaged in our nation is growing all over America.

When I announced I was going to run for president, I said that it would take a political revolution for the junior senator from Vermont to win the presidency. A lot of pundits thought that was an acknowledgment of impossibility. It wasn't. It was a statement of what would be necessary to undo the damage that has been done and to reclaim our country from the oligarchs. The pundits and the political consultants still have a hard time understanding this. But the people get it. They are turning out by the thousands, by the tens of thousands, for our rallies. They are sending contributions of $5 or $10 because they understand that if we all give what we can, then we might yet be able to beat the billionaire class.

I decided to run for president because I believed it was necessary to do so, because I believed that this campaign could bring about a political revolution, and I believed we could win. We did it in Burlington. We did it in Vermont. And we are doing it in America. Change comes, even in the face of overwhelming odds. And the recognition of the changes we have already made, of what we have won, inspires us to fight even harder.

If we don't stand together today, working Americans will continue fighting an uphill battle just to make ends meet at the end of each month. We cannot settle for establishment politics and stale ideas. Now is the time to transform America.

That's what I believe from the bottom of my heart.

SENATOR BERNIE SANDERS
Burlington, Vermont
October 2015

The Economy

(Senate–December 10, 2010)

Mr. SANDERS. Mr. President, as I think everyone knows, President Obama and the Republican leadership have reached an agreement on a very significant tax bill. In my view, the agreement they reached is a bad deal for the American people. I think we can do better.

I am here today to take a strong stand against this bill, and I intend to tell my colleagues and the Nation exactly why I am in opposition to this bill. You can call what I am doing today whatever you want. You can call it a filibuster. You can call it a very long speech. I am not here to set any great records or to make a spectacle; I am simply here today to take as long as I can to explain to the American people the fact that we have to do a lot better than this agreement provides.

Let me enumerate some of the reasons I am opposed to this agreement.

First, as everybody knows, this Nation has a record-breaking $13.8 trillion national debt at the same time as the middle class is collapsing and poverty is increasing. And I think it is important to say a word—because I am not necessarily sure a lot of Americans know this—about how we got to where we are today in terms of the national debt.

I know there are some people who think this all began the day President Obama took office. Well, that is not quite the case. When President Clinton left office, this country was running, in fact, a very significant surplus, and the projections were that we were going to continue to run a surplus. During the eight years of President Bush's administration, for a number of reasons—the primary reasons being the war in Iraq, the war in Afghanistan, huge tax breaks for the wealthiest people in this country, a Medicare Part D prescription drug program, the Wall Street bailout, among other things, all of which were not paid for—we saw an almost doubling of the national debt. Since President Obama has been in office, we have passed a stimulus package which has also added to the deficit and national debt.

But here we are today with a $13.8 trillion national debt, a $1.3 trillion deficit, and almost all Americans are in agreement that this is a very serious issue. So the first point I would make is that it seems to me to be unconscionable—unconscionable—for my conservative friends to be driving up this already too high national debt by giving tax breaks to millionaires and billionaires who don't need it, and in a number of cases they don't even want it.

Here is one of the interesting ironies. There are lists of many very wealthy people who have come forward and said: Sure, I want a tax break. Everybody wants a tax break. But you know what, there are other priorities in this country, and I don't need it. Two of the wealthiest people in the world— and these are billionaires—Bill Gates of Microsoft and Warren Buffett of Berkshire, say: It is absurd. We don't need a tax break.

All over the country, you hear a lot of folks who have a lot of money saying: Don't drive up the deficit and force our kids to pay higher taxes to pay off the national debt in order to give tax breaks to the richest people in this country.

We have been told not to worry too much because the extension of these tax breaks for the wealthy will only last two years—not to worry. Maybe that is the case. But given the political reality I have seen in Washington, my guess is that two years from now these tax breaks for the wealthiest people in this country will be extended again. What happens around here is that the argument will be made that if you end these tax breaks you are raising taxes. That is what we are hearing right now. I see no reason why, in the middle of a Presidential election, those arguments will not be made again and I see no reason not to believe that those tax breaks will be extended again.

(The ACTING PRESIDENT pro tempore assumed the chair.)

Mr. SANDERS. Clearly, we have a number of Republicans who want to make that extension permanent. Whether it will ever be made permanent I don't know. But the point is, when you hear folks say it is only a two-year extension, I suggest you take that with a grain of salt.

Let me say, if in fact we do what the Republicans have wanted to do right now as we enter this debate—they wanted a 10-year extension—that would add $700 billion to our national debt. I have four kids and I have six grandchildren. None of them has a whole lot of money. I think it is grossly unfair to ask my kids and grandchildren and the children all over this country to be paying higher taxes in order to provide tax breaks for billionaires because we have driven up the national debt. That is plain wrong. I think the vast majority of the American people, whether they are progressives like myself or whether they are conservatives, perceive that concept of giving tax breaks to billionaires when we have such a high national debt makes no sense at all.

Furthermore, it is important to point out that extending income tax breaks to the top 2 percent is not the only unfair tax proposal in this agreement. This agreement between the President and the Republican leadership also calls for a continuation of the Bush-era 15 percent tax rate on capital gains and dividends, meaning that those people who make their living off their investments will continue to pay a substantially lower tax rate than firemen, teachers, nurses, carpenters, and virtually all the other working people of this country. I do not think that is fair. That is wrong. If this agreement were to be passed, we would be continuing that unfair arrangement.

On top of all that, this agreement includes a horrendous proposal regarding the estate tax. That is a Teddy Roosevelt initiative. Teddy Roosevelt was talking about this in the early years of the 20th century. It was enacted in 1916 and it was enacted for a couple of reasons. Teddy Roosevelt and the people of that era thought it was wrong that a handful of people could have a huge concentration of wealth and then give that wealth, transmit that wealth to their children tax free. He did not think that was right.

Furthermore, it was a source, a progressive and fair source, of revenue. Under the agreement struck between the Republican leadership and the President, the estate tax rate, which was 55 percent on the value of estates over $1 million under President Clinton—and let's all remember, we had problems with the economy under President Clinton but very few will deny that during those years we were creating a heck of a lot more jobs than we did under President Bush. That is the fact—over 20 million jobs were created under President Clinton. We lost over 600,000 private sector jobs under President Bush. During the Clinton era, the estate tax rate was 55 percent on the value of estates over $1 million. What this arrangement would do is lower that tax rate to 35 percent, with an exemption on the first $5 million of an individual's estate and $10 million for couples.

Here is the important point I think many people do not know. I have to confess my Republican friends and their pollsters and their language people have done a very good job. This is the so-called death tax. I think all over America people say this is terrible. I have $50,000 in the bank and I want to leave that to my kids and the Government is going to take 55 percent of that, 35 percent of that. What an outrage.

Let us be very clear: This tax applies only—only—to the top three-tenths of 1 percent of American families; 99.7 percent of American families will not pay one nickel in an estate tax. This is not a tax on the rich, this is a tax on the very, very, very rich.

If my Republican friends had been successful in doing what they want to do, which is eliminate this estate tax completely, it would have cost our Treasury—raised the national debt by some $1 trillion over a 10-year period. Families such as the Walton family, of Walmart fame, would have received, just this one family, about a $30 billion tax break.

I find it hard to believe when we are talking about massive cuts in programs for working families, when we have this huge national debt, that anybody would be agreeing to lowering the estate tax rate to 35 percent with a $5 million exemption. That is what this agreement does and I think that is a very bad idea.

Once again, while the agreement on the estate tax is for two years—once again, there is very little doubt in my mind that the Republicans will continue to push for lower and lower estate tax rates because that is what they want. I think

Senator *Kyl* has been pretty clear about this. They want to permanently repeal that tax. That would add about $1 trillion to the national debt over a ten-year period and would only benefit the top three-tenths of 1 percent. I think we are down a bad path there and that is another reason why this agreement does not make a whole lot of sense.

Third—and this is a very important point that I think has not yet gotten the attention it deserves—this agreement contains a payroll tax holiday which would cut $120 billion from Social Security payroll taxes for workers. There are a lot of folks out there who say: This is pretty good. I am a worker, my contribution will go from 6.2 percent today down to 4.2 percent. I will have more money in my paycheck. It is a good idea.

Let's take a deep breath and let's think about it for a second and understand what this whole thing is about. This payroll tax holiday concept, as I understand it, originally started with conservative Republicans. I know the Vice President recently made the point this was originally a Republican idea. Why did the Republicans come up with this idea? These are exactly the same people who do not believe in Social Security. These are the same people who either want to make significant cuts in Social Security or else they want to privatize Social Security entirely. Here is the point: They understand that if we divert funding that is supposed to go into the Social Security trust fund, which is what this payroll tax holiday does, this is money that goes into the Social Security trust fund that is now being diverted, cut back, in order to provide financial support for workers—but that is a lot of money not going into the trust fund.

What the President and others are saying is not to worry because that money will be covered by the general fund. That is a very bad and dangerous precedent. Up until now, what Social Security has been about is 100 percent funding from payroll contributions, not from the general tax base. Once again, this is a one-year program. The loss of revenue going into Social Security can be covered by the general fund. But we have a $13.8 trillion national debt. How much longer will the general fund put money into Social Security? Is it a good idea for the general fund to be doing that?

I would argue this is not a good idea. This is a very danger-ous step forward for those of us who believe in Social Security. But this is not just *Bernie Sanders* saying this. One of the more effective and I think important senior groups in America is called the National Committee to Preserve Social Security and Medicare. I don't know exactly how many but they have many members all over this country. I know they are active in the State of Vermont. I want to read to you from a press release they sent out the other day. This is the headline on it, from the National Committee to Preserve Social Security and Medi-care: "Cutting Contributions to Social Security Signals the Be-ginning of the End. Payroll Tax Holiday Is Anything But."

This is what they say. This comes from Barbara Kennelly. Barbara came from the House of Representatives. I have known her for years. She is now the president and CEO of the National Committee to Preserve Social Security and Medi-care, one of the strongest senior groups in the country.

"Even though Social Security contributed nothing to the current economic crisis, it has been bartered in a deal that provides deficit-busting tax cuts for the wealthy. Diverting $120 billion in Social Security contributions for a so-called 'tax holiday' may sound like a good deal for workers now, but it's bad business for the program that a majority of middle-class seniors will rely upon in the future."

That is what the National Committee to Preserve Social Security and Medicare says about that agreement and I agree with them. For all of us who understand that Social Security is life and death for tens of millions of Americans today and will be vitally important for working people as they reach retirement age, it is important that we understand that Social Security has done a great job. A few minutes ago the Presiding Officer was on the floor talking about the strong work that our Federal employees do, and he is absolutely right. Sometimes we also take for granted that Social Security has been an enormous success. It has done exactly what those people who created it have wanted it to do—nothing more, nothing less. It has succeeded. It has taken millions of seniors out of poverty and given them an element of security. It has also helped people with disabilities maintain their dignity. Widows and orphans are also getting help.

For 75 years it has worked well. It has a $2.6 trillion surplus today and it can pay out benefits for the next 27 years. It is strong. We want to make it stronger. This payroll tax holiday I am afraid is a step very much in the wrong direction and that is one of the important reasons why this agreement between the President and the Republicans should be defeated.

Included in the agreement are a number of business tax cuts. I am not going to say that some of them may not work. Some of them may work. Some will work better than others. There is a whole list of them. But this is what I will say. Economists on both ends of the political spectrum believe that if we are serious about addressing the horrendous economic crisis we are in now, 9.8 percent unemployment, there are far more effective ways of creating the jobs we have to create than those tax proposals. With corporate America already sitting on close to $2 trillion cash on hand, it is not that our friends in corporate America don't have any money, we have to help them. They have $2 trillion cash on hand. The problem is not in my view that corporate taxes are too high; it is that the middle class simply doesn't have the money to purchase the goods and products that make our economy go and create jobs.

I think if our goal is to create the millions and millions of jobs we need, and if our goal is to make our country stronger internationally in a very tough global economy, I would much prefer, and I think most economists would agree with me that a better way to do that, to create the millions of jobs we have to create, is to invest heavily in our infrastructure.

The truth is—and I don't think anyone disputes this, the infrastructure in the United States is crumbling, and I will go into more detail about that later.

I have some very good information on it. But you do not have to be a civil engineer to know that. All you have to do is get in your car today and drive someplace in my state and all over this country. What you are going to see are roads that are in disrepair. You are going to see bridges that, in some cases, have actually been shut down. You are going to see water systems—I remember I was in Rutland, Vermont, the second or third largest city in the State of Vermont, and the mayor showed me a piece of pipe, an old piece of pipe.

He said: You know, the engineer who helped develop this water system and lay this pipe, after he did this work for Rutland, he went off to fight in the war.

I knew there was a catch line coming. I said: What war was it?

He said: It was the Civil War.

So you are talking about water pipe being in Rutland, Vermont—and this is true all over the United States—laid in the Civil War. The result is, we lose an enormous amount of clean water every day through leaks and water pipes bursting all over the United States of America.

Well, we can put people to work improving our water systems, our wastewater plants. It is a very expensive proposition to develop a good wastewater plant. I was a mayor, you were a Governor, Mr. President. It is an expensive proposition for roads, bridges. Furthermore, I do not have to tell anybody here, our rail system, which used to be the greatest rail system in the world, is now falling way behind every other major country on Earth.

As a result of the stimulus package, we did a whole lot of very good things in the State of Vermont. One of the things we were able to do was use $50 million of Federal funds and private money to make major repairs on one of our important railways in the state.

But we remain far behind most other countries around the industrialized world. China is exploding in terms of the number of high-speed rail lines they have. We have to do better. Our airports need work. Our air control systems need to be updated in terms of the technology they need to make our flights safe.

The point is, what most economists would tell you is when you invest in infrastructure, you get a bigger bang for the buck. You create more jobs for your investment than, in most instances, giving a variety of tax breaks to the corporate world.

Second of all, and not unimportantly, when you invest in infrastructure, you are improving the future of this country. You are making us more productive. It is not just creating jobs, it is creating jobs for very specific purposes, which makes our Nation more productive and efficient.

Thirdly, let me tell you something. As a former mayor, infrastructure does not get better if you ignore it. You can turn your back, if you are a mayor or Governor, on the roads and the highways because you do not have the money to fix them today, but they are not going to get better next year. At some point, they are going to have to be repaired and fixed. We may as well do that right now.

So I believe the money, the very substantial sums of money in this agreement between the President and the Republicans, which goes into tax breaks for corporate America, could be more effectively spent on infrastructure.

The fifth point I want to make in opposition to this agreement and what we have heard from the President and others, is that this is a compromise. You cannot get everything you want. Well, you cannot get everything you want around here that is true, but one of the examples of this compromise is an extension of unemployment benefits for 13 months.

Well, let me be very clear. In the midst of a serious and major recession, at a time when millions of our fellow Americans are not only out of work through no fault of their own, but they have been out of work for a very long time, it would be, in my view, immoral and wrong to turn our backs on those workers. Their unemployment benefits are going to be running out soon. It is absolutely imperative that we extend those unemployment benefits for the 2 million workers who would lose them.

But here is the point I want to make. Some people say this is a compromise. Well, the Republicans gave ground on unemployment; the President gave ground on extending tax breaks for the rich, et cetera. But here is the point. I do not believe, honestly, that the Republican support now for extending unemployment benefits constitutes much of a compromise because the truth is, for the past 40 years, under both Democratic and Republican administrations, under the leadership in the Senate and the House by Democrats or

Republicans, it has been bipartisan policy that whenever the unemployment rate has been above 7.2 percent, unemployment insurance has always been extended. So what we have had is longstanding, bipartisan policy. That is what we have always done. That is what we should be doing in the future. I do not regard Republicans now supporting what their party has always supported, extending unemployment benefits when unemployment becomes very high—I do not see that as a compromise. I see that as what has been going on in this country and in the Senate for four decades.

I have talked about the negative aspects of this proposal. But I am going to be the first to admit that, of course, there are positive and good agreements in this. And what are they? What are some of the positive aspects of this agreement? Let me just tick them off.

Number One, I believe very strongly, and I know the President does, it is absolutely imperative that we extend middle-class tax cuts for 98 percent of the American workforce. I do not think there has been any debate about that.

When median family income has gone down by over $2,000 during the Bush years, when millions of our people today are working longer hours for low wages, when people cannot afford to send their kids to college or to take care of childcare, I think it makes absolute sense. I do not think anyone will argue it is absolutely imperative that we extend middle-class tax cuts. That is what this provision does. That is the right thing.

Furthermore, in this agreement we have an extension of the earned-income tax credit for working Americans, and the child and college tax credit extensions are also in there. Every one of these agreements is very important. These programs will keep millions of Americans from slipping out of the middle class and into poverty. They will allow millions of Americans to send their kids to college.

So I am not here to say there is not anything of value in this agreement between the President and the Republicans. There are, and we have to fight to make sure all of those programs remain in the final package when it is passed—when the final package is passed. But when we look at the overall agreement, we must put it in a broader context; that is, what will the passage of this legislation mean for the future of our country?

In that area, if you look at it in that context, I think the evidence is pretty strong it is not a good agreement and not something that should be passed. The passage of this agreement would mean we would continue the Bush policy of trickle-down economics for at least two more years. That is not a good thing to do because, I think, as most Americans know, that philosophy, that economic approach, simply did not work. The evidence is quite overwhelming. I do not think there is much debate, when median family income during Bush's eight years goes down by $2,200, when we end up losing over 600,000 private sector jobs, and all of the job growth was in the government sector, I do not see how anybody would want to continue that philosophy. But that, in essence, is what will happen if this agreement is passed.

Now, I want to make another point about what happens if—if, and I will do my best to prevent this from happening—but what would happen if this agreement would pass? Does anybody seriously believe our Republican colleagues would then say: OK, well, we have an extension of tax breaks for the very richest people. We have lowered the tax rate on the estate tax. Those are good victories for millionaires and billionaires. We are going to go home now. We are not going to continue the fight.

I do not think so. We are already hearing sounds about where our Republican friends want to go. The President put together what I thought was a very poor deficit reduction commission. I thought the folks on it were not reflective of the American people. I thought there was very much a big business, corporate partiality there.

The initiatives that came out of that commission—which, fortunately, did not get the 14 votes they needed—suggest to me that those of us who are concerned about protecting the needs of the middle class and working families are going to have to push back pretty hard for what is coming down the pike.

I think what we will be seeing is—if this proposal negotiated between the President and the Republicans is passed, what you will be seeing within a few months are folks coming on the floor of the Senate, and this is what they will say: "You know what? The deficit is high. The national debt is too high. And, yes—oh, yes—we drove the national debt up by giving tax breaks to millionaires. That is the way it goes. But we are going to have to deal with our national debt."

The Republicans will tell you: "Oh, we have a great plan to deal with it. We are giving tax breaks to millionaires. But now what we are going to have to do is start making deep cuts in Social Security, and that deficit reduction commission started paving the way for that, very substantial cuts in Social Security."

Maybe we will have to raise the retirement age in Social Security to 69 or 70. Maybe we will have to make cuts in Medicare. Maybe we will have to make cuts in Medicaid. I think we are beginning to see, in the State of Arizona now, what goes on when you make deep cuts in Medicaid.

In Arizona right now there are people who are in line who need transplants, who will die if they do not get transplants, as a result of legislation they passed there. They are saying to people, young people: Sorry, we cannot afford to give you a transplant, and you are going to have to die.

Well, is that what we are looking forward to saying all over America? I certainly will do everything I can to prevent that.

We are certainly going to see attacks on environmental protection, on education. Some of us believe if this country is going to prosper and succeed in the global economy, we have to have the best educational system in the world from childcare through college.

Right now, it is extremely difficult for middle-class families to send their kids to college. Does anyone have any doubt whatsoever that our Republican friends are not going to come back here and say: Oh, we cannot afford to raise Pell Grants as we have in recent years. We cannot afford to support working families who have their kids in childcare. Cut. Cut. Cut.

That is insanity. I am being honest about it. So I would suggest their argument is that we have a high deficit and a high national debt; that if we pass this agreement and the national debt goes higher, it only gives them more impetus to go forward to cut programs that benefit working families and the middle class.

Let me also say there is no doubt in my mind what many—not all but many—of my Republican colleagues want to do; that is, they want to move this country back into the 1920s when essentially we had an economic and political system which was controlled by big money interests; where working people and the middle class had no programs to sustain them when things got bad, when they got old, and when they got sick; when labor unions were very hard to come by because of antiworker legislation. That is what they want. They do not believe in things like the Environmental Protection Agency. They do not believe in things like Social Security, Medicare, Medicaid, Federal aid to education. That is the fight we will be waging.

I think to surrender on this issue is to simply say we are going to be waging fight after fight, starting within a couple of months.

President Obama has said he fought as hard as he could against the Republican tax breaks for the wealthy and for an extension in unemployment. Well, maybe. But the reality is that fight cannot simply be waged inside the Beltway. Our job is to appeal to the vast majority of the American people to stand up and to say: Wait a minute. I do not want to see our national debt explode. I do not want to see my kids and grandchildren paying higher taxes in order to give tax breaks to millionaires and billionaires.

The vast majority of the American people do not support that agreement in terms of giving tax breaks to the very rich. Our job is to rally those people. I would like very much to see the American people saying to our Republican colleagues and some Democratic colleagues: Excuse me. Don't force my kids to have a lower standard of living in order to give tax breaks to the richest people.

What the President and all of us should be doing is going out and saying to those people: Call the Members of the Senate, call the Members of the House and say: Excuse me. How about representing the middle class and working families, for a change, rather than the wealthiest people. That is what democracy is about.

This fight is not going to be won inside the Beltway in a Senate debate. It is going to be won when the American people stand and say: Wait a second. We cannot continue to give tax breaks to people who are doing phenomenally well right now. We cannot give tax breaks to the rich when we already have the most unequal distribution of income of any major country on Earth. In 2007, the top 1 percent earned 23.5 percent of all income in America, more than the bottom 50 percent. They don't need more tax breaks to be paid for by our kids and grandchildren.

The vast majority of people are behind us on this issue, but they have to make their voices heard to their Senators, to their Congressmen. When they do, I believe we can come forward with an agreement which protects the middle-class and working families and is not a boondoggle for the wealthiest people.

It is important to put the agreement the President struck with Republicans in a broader context. We can't just look at the agreement unto itself. We have to look at it within the context of what is going on in the country today, both economically and politically. I think I speak for millions of Americans. There is a war going on in this country. I am not referring to the war in Iraq or the war in Afghanistan. I am talking about a war being waged by some of the wealthiest and most powerful people against working families, against the disappearing and shrinking middle class of our country. The billionaires of America are on the warpath. They want more and more and more. That has everything to do with this agreement reached between Republicans and the President.

In 2007, the top 1 percent of all income earners made 23.5 percent of all income. Let me repeat that: The top 1 percent earned over 23 percent of all income; that is, more than the bottom 50 percent. One percent here; fifty percent here. But for the very wealthy, that is apparently not enough. The percentage of income going to the top 1 percent nearly tripled since the 1970s. All over this country people are angry, frustrated. It is true in Vermont. I am sure it is true in Virginia. It is true all over America. But one of the reasons people are angry and frustrated is they are working incredibly hard. In Vermont, I can tell my colleagues, there are people who don't work one job, two jobs; there are people working three jobs and four jobs, trying to cobble together an income in order to support their families. I suspect that goes on all across the country. While people are working harder and harder, in many cases their income is going down. The fact is, 80 percent of all new income earned from 1980 to 2005 has gone to the top 1 percent. Let me repeat that because that is an important fact. It explains why the American people are feeling as angry as they are. They are working hard, but they are not going anyplace. In some cases, in many cases, their standard of living is actually going down. Eighty percent of all income in recent years has gone to the top 1 percent. The richer people become much richer, the middle class shrinks. Millions of Americans fall out of the middle class and into poverty.

That is not apparently enough for our friends at the top who have a religious ferocity in terms of greed. They need more, more. It is similar to an addiction. Fifty million is not enough. They need $100 million. One hundred million is not enough; they need $1 billion. One billion is not enough. I am not quite sure how much they need. When will it stop?

Today, in terms of wealth as opposed to income, the top 1 percent now owns more wealth than the bottom 90 percent.

When we went to school, we used to read in the textbooks about Latin America, and they used to refer to some of the countries there as "banana republics," countries in which a handful of families controlled the economic and political life of the nation. I don't wish to upset the American people, but we are not all that far away from that reality today. The top 1 percent has seen a tripling of the percentage of income they earn. In 2007, the top 1 percent earned 23.5 percent of all income, more than the bottom 50 percent. The top 1 percent now owns more wealth than the bottom 90 percent. That is not the foundation of a democratic society. That is the foundation for an oligarchic society. The rich get richer. The middle class shrinks. Poverty increases. Apparently, good is not good enough yet for some of the richest people.

I say "some of the richest" because there are a lot of folks with a lot of money who do love this country, they are not into greed, but there are some who are. More, more more, that is what they need.

For example—this galls me and galls many of the people in this country—the horrendous recession we are in right now, where millions and millions of people have lost their jobs, their savings, their homes, this recession was caused by the greed and recklessness and illegal behavior on Wall Street. These guys, through their greed, created the most severe economic recession since the Great Depression. The American people bailed them out. Now, two years after the bailout, they are giving themselves more compensation than they ever have. They are saying to the American people: Sorry we caused this recession because of our greed. Sorry you are unemployed. Sorry you lost your house. But that is not all that important. What is important is that I, on Wall Street, continue to get millions of dollars in compensation and in bonuses, that I have big parties. How can I get by on one house? I need 5 houses, 10 houses. I need three jet planes to take me all over the world. Sorry. We have the money. We have the power. We have the lobbyists here on Wall Street. Tough luck. That is the world, get used to it.

The rich get richer. The middle class shrinks. Not enough, not enough. The very rich seem to want more and more and more, and they are prepared to dismantle the existing political and social order in order to get it. So we have the economics and distribution of income and wealth as one thing, but then we must discuss politics.

What happened last year, as I think most Americans know, is the Supreme Court made a very strange decision. The Supreme Court decided that corporations are people and they have the right of free speech and the right without disclosure—all of this is through the *Citizens United* Supreme Court decision—to put as much money as they want into campaigns all over the country. In this last campaign, that is what we saw: Billionaires, in secret, pouring money into campaigns all over the country. Does that sound like democracy to anybody in America; that we have a handful of billionaires probably dividing up the country? I will put this amount in Virginia, California, wherever.

That is what they were able to do. The rich get richer, and they don't sit on this money. What they then do is use it to elect people who support them and to unelect people who oppose their agenda and they use their political power to get legislation passed which makes the wealthy even wealthier.

One of the manifestations of that is, in fact, the agreement reached between the President and the Republican leadership. The wealthy contribute huge sums of money into campaigns. The wealthy have all kinds of lobbyists around here through corporate America. What they are going to get out of this agreement are huge tax breaks that benefit themselves. That is not what we should be supporting.

We should understand this agreement is just the beginning of an assault on legislation and programs that have benefited the American people for 70 or 80 years. Mark my words, there will be an intensive effort to privatize Social Security and Medicare and Medicaid. Furthermore, it is part of the Republican agenda. They want to expand—and it is not only Republicans here, some Democrats as well—our disastrous trade policies so large companies can continue their efforts to outsource American jobs to China and other low-wage countries. Any objective analysis of our trade policies has shown it has been a grotesque failure for ordinary Americans. It is hard to calculate exactly, but I think it is fair to say we have lost millions of decent-paying jobs. Since 2001, some 42,000 factories shut down. We went from 17 million manufacturing jobs to less than 12 million manufacturing jobs. Historically, in this country, manufacturing jobs were the backbone of the working class. That is how people made it into the middle class. That is how they had decent health care benefits and pensions. Every day we are seeing those jobs disappear because corporate America would prefer to do business in China or other low-wage countries.

I returned from a trip to Vietnam last year, a beautiful country. People there work for 25, 30 cents an hour. Sometimes when you go to a store, you may see a shirt made in Bangladesh. That shirt, in all likelihood, is made by a young girl who came in from the countryside to one of the factories there. The good news is that in Bangladesh, the minimum wage was doubled. It went from 11 cents an hour to 22 cents an hour.

Are American workers going to be able to compete against desperate people who make 22 cents an hour?

So my view—and I think it reflects the views of the American people—is that of course we want to see the people of Bangladesh and the people of China do well. But they do not have to do well at the expense of the American middle class. We do not have to engage in a race to the bottom. Our goal is to bring them up, not take us down. But one of the results of our disastrous trade policies is that in many instances wages in the United States have gone down.

I believe in the coming months you are going to see an intensification of efforts to expand unfettered free trade. I think that will be a continuation of a disastrous policy for American workers.

Let me personalize this a little bit. This gentleman, shown in this picture I have in the Chamber—I have no personal animus toward him at all; I think I met him once in a large room.

His name is James Dimon. He is the CEO of JPMorgan Chase. Over the past five years, Mr. Dimon, who is the CEO of JP-Morgan Chase, received $110 million in total compensation—a bank that we now know received hundreds of billions in low-interest loans and other financial assistance from the Federal Reserve and the Treasury Department.

So Mr. Dimon received $110 million in total compensation over the past five years. His bank was bailed out big time by the taxpayers. But under the legislation the President negotiated with the Republicans, Mr. Dimon—I use him just as one example of thousands; nothing personal to Mr. Dimon—will receive $1.1 million in tax breaks. So $1.1 million in tax breaks for a major CEO on Wall Street, who over the last five years received $110 million in total compensation.

Meanwhile—just to contrast what is going on here—two days ago, I brought before the Senate legislation which would provide a $250 one-time check to over 50 million seniors and disabled veterans, who for the last two years have not received a COLA in their Social Security benefits. Many of those seniors and disabled vets are trying to get by on $14,000, $15,000, $18,000 a year. The total package for that bill was approximately $14 billion that would go out to over 50 million seniors and disabled vets. We won that vote on the floor of the Senate 53 to 45. But just because you get 53 votes in the Senate does not mean you win. Because the Republicans filibustered, I needed 60 votes. I could not get 60 votes. I could not get one Republican vote to provide a $250 check to a disabled veteran trying to get by on $15,000 or $16,000 a year.

But Mr. Dimon, who made $110 million in the last five years, will get a $1.1 million tax break if this agreement is passed. Now, that may make sense to some people. It does not make a lot of sense to me.

Again, I have no particular knowledge, animus—I do not know if I ever met John Mack in my life. He is the CEO of Morgan Stanley. In 2006, he received a $40 million bonus, which at the time was the largest bonus ever given to a Wall Street executive.

Two years after receiving this bonus, Morgan Stanley received some $2 trillion in low-interest loans and billions from the Treasury Department. Instead of losing his job, under this agreement, Mr. Mack will be receiving an estimated $926,000 tax break next year. Congratulations, Mr. Mack. You are doing fine. We could not get $250 for a disabled vet.

Over the past five years, Ken Lewis, the former CEO of Bank of America, received over $147 million in total compensation. In 2008, Bank of America received hundreds of billions in taxpayer-backed loans from the Fed and a $45 billion bailout from the Treasury Department.

What will Mr. Lewis receive if the agreement negotiated between the President and the Republicans goes forth? He will get a $713,000 tax cut.

And on and on it goes. I did not mean to specifically pick on these guys. Some of the wealthiest people in the country will be receiving a million-dollar-plus tax break. So we as a Nation have to decide whether that makes a lot of sense. I think it does not.

Let me mention that a couple weeks ago the Fed, the Federal Reserve, published on their Web site some 21,000 loans and other transactions it made during the Wall Street meltdown period. That disclosure was made possible as part of a provision that I put into the financial reform bill because I thought it was important that we, for the first time, lift the veil of secrecy at the Fed and get a sense of the kind of money that was lent out by the Fed and who received that money.

What is very interesting is that the American people and the media have focused on the $700 billion Wall Street bailout now known as TARP. I happen to have voted against that agreement, but, in fairness, that agreement was pretty transparent. The Treasury Department put up on their Web site all of those banks and financial institutions that received the money. If you want to know where the money went, it is right up there on the Treasury Department's Web site.

But at the same time, a bigger transaction than TARP was taking place, which got relatively little attention, and that was the role the Fed was playing in terms of the Wall Street bailout.

While the TARP issue was being debated during that period, Ben Bernanke, the Chairman of the Federal Reserve, Tim Geithner, who was then the president of the New York Fed, and a handful of other very powerful people were sitting behind closed doors getting ready to lend out trillions—underline trillions—of taxpayer dollars to large financial institutions and corporations, with no debate going on in Congress, no debate whatsoever.

On March 3, 2009—and I am a member of the Senate Budget Committee—I asked the Fed Chairman, Mr. Bernanke, to tell the American people the names of the financial institutions that received this unprecedented backdoor bailout from the Fed, how much they received, and the exact terms of this assistance. I will never forget that. I asked Mr. Bernanke for that information. He said: Senator, no, not going to give it to you, not going to make it public.

Well, on that day, I introduced legislation to make that information public, working with a number of Members of the House and the Senate. Some strange bedfellows—conservatives and progressives—came together on this issue. We managed to get in the Wall Street reform bill a disclosure provision, and on December 1—last week—that information was made public. Let me talk a little bit about what was in that information made public by the Fed.

After years of stonewalling, the American people have learned the incredible, jaw-dropping details of the Fed's multi-trillion-dollar bailout of Wall Street and corporate America—not just Wall Street. It is one of the things we learned. As a result of this disclosure, in my view—we are going to get into what was in what we learned—Congress has to take a very extensive look at all aspects of how the Federal Reserve functions and how we can make our financial institutions more responsive to the needs of ordinary Americans and small businesses.

What have we learned from the disclosure of December 1? This is based on an examination of over 21,000 separate Federal Reserve transactions. More work, more research needs to be done. But this is what we have learned so far.

As it turns out, while small business owners in the State of Vermont and throughout this country were being turned down for loans, not only did large financial institutions—and I am talking about every major financial institution—receive substantial help from the Fed, but also some of the largest corporations in this country—not financial institutions—also received help in terms of very low interest loans.

So you have every major financial institution, you have some of our largest private corporations, but here is something we also learned, and that is that this bailout impacted not just American banks and corporations but also foreign banks and foreign corporations as well, to the tune of many billions of dollars.

Then, on top of that, a number of the wealthiest individuals in this country also received a major bailout from the Fed. The "emergency response," which is what the Fed described their action as during the Wall Street collapse, appears to any objective observer to have been the clearest case that I can imagine of socialism for the very rich and rugged free market capitalism for everybody else.

In other words, if you are a huge financial institution, whose recklessness and greed caused this great recession, no problem. You are going to receive a substantial amount of help from the taxpayers of this country. If you are a major American corporation, such as General Electric or McDonald's or Caterpillar or Harley-Davidson or Verizon, no problem. You are going to receive a major handout from the U.S. Government.

But if you are a small business in Vermont or California or Virginia, well, guess what, you are on your own because right now we know one of the real impediments to the kind of job creation we need in this country is that small businesses are not getting the loans they need.

Furthermore, what we now know is the extent of the bailout for the large financial corporations. Goldman Sachs received nearly $780 billion. Morgan Stanley received over $2 trillion. Citigroup received $2.4 trillion. Bear Stearns received nearly $1 trillion. And Merrill Lynch received $2.2 trillion in short-term loans from the Fed.

But I think what is most surprising for the American people is not just the bailout of Wall Street and the financial institutions, and the bailout of large American corporations such as General Electric, but I think the American people would find it very strange that at a time when the American automobile sector was on the verge of collapse—and goodness only knows how many thousands and thousands of jobs we have lost in automobile manufacturing in this country—the Federal Reserve was also bailing out Toyota and Mitsubishi, two Asian carmakers, by purchasing nearly $5 billion worth of their commercial paper from November 5, 2008, through January 30, 2009.

While virtually no American-made cars or products of any kind are bought in Japan, I think the American people would be shocked to learn that the Fed extended over $380 billion to the Central Bank of Japan to bail out banks in that country.

Furthermore, I think the American people are interested to know that the Fed bailed out the Korea Development Bank, the wholly owned, state-owned Bank of South Korea, by purchasing over $2 billion of its commercial paper. The sole purpose of the Korea Development Bank is to finance and manage major industrial projects to enhance the national economy not of the United States of America but of South Korea. I am not against South Korea. I wish the South Koreans all the luck in the world. But it should not be the taxpayers of the United States lending their banks' money to create jobs in South Korea. I would suggest maybe we want to create jobs in the United States of America. At the same time, the Fed also extended over $40 billion for the Central Bank of South Korea so that it had enough money to bail out its own banks.

At a time when small businesses in Vermont and all over this country cannot get the loans they need to expand their businesses, I think the American people would find it extremely—I don't know what the word is—maybe amusing that the Fed bailed out the state-owned Bank of Bavaria—not Pennsylvania, not California, but Bavaria—by purchasing over $2.2 billion of its commercial paper.

Furthermore, when we cannot get support on the floor of this Senate to extend unemployment benefits to millions of Americans who are on the verge of seeing them expire, I think the American people would find it incomprehensible that the Fed chose to bail out the Arab Banking Corporation based in Bahrain by providing them with over $23 billion in loans with an interest rate as low as one-quarter of 1 percent. So small businessmen all over America: Maybe you have to run to Bahrain and work with the Arab Banking Corporation there to get some pretty good loans. But it would be nice if maybe the Fed would start to pay attention to the needs of the middle class in this country.

Furthermore, the Fed extended over $9.6 billion to the Central Bank of Mexico.

What is interesting about all of this is that we had a very vigorous debate here in the Senate and in the House over the $700 billion TARP program. Every person in America could turn on C-SPAN and hear that debate. They could hear what President Bush had to say, hear what then-Senator Obama and Senator *McCain* had to say. It was all pretty public. But what took place at the Fed, which, in fact, amounted to a larger bailout, was done behind closed doors. Over $3 trillion was lent with zero transparency. In fact, as a result of this recent disclosure—this is the first time we have gotten a glimpse of the magnitude and the particulars, the specificities of where that money was lent, and I think this is a good thing for this country. Again, I voted against the bailout of Wall Street, but the debate was open and public. People wrote to their Senators and called their Senators. That is called democracy. After the TARP bailout took place, all of the loans were put up on the Web site. Transparency—the American people knew who got the money. But the actions of the Fed were done behind closed doors, and, in my view—it is an issue we are studying right now—I think there were significant conflicts of interest. I think we had people sitting there at the New York Fed who were beneficiaries of this bailout, and that is an issue we need to explore. I should tell my colleagues that as part of the provision we got into the financial reform bill, the GAO is, in fact, doing just that—investigating possible conflicts of interest at the Fed with regard to this bailout.

I think the question the American people are asking as they read about what the Fed did during the financial crisis is whether the Fed has now become the central bank of the world without any debate on the floor of the Senate or the Congress and without the knowledge of the American people. I think that is wrong. So I hope, out of this effort in bringing disclosure and transparency to the Fed, that one of the things that will come will be more transparency at the Fed.

As I indicated a moment ago, the Fed said this bailout was necessary in order to prevent the world economy from going over a cliff. But three years after the start of the recession, millions of Americans remain unemployed and have lost their homes, their life savings, and their ability to send their kids to college. Meanwhile, huge banks and large corporations have returned to making incredible profits and paying their executives recordbreaking compensation packages, as if the financial crisis they started never occurred.

What this recent disclosure tells us, among many other things, is that despite this huge taxpayer bailout, the Fed did not make the appropriate demands on these financial institutions which would have been necessary to rebuild our economy and protect the needs of ordinary Americans. In other words, what they simply did was give out billions and billions of dollars which were used in the self-interests of these financial institutions rather than saying: The American people who are hurting are bailing you out, and now that they have bailed you out, your responsibility is to do what you can to create jobs and to improve the standard of living of the people, many of whose lives you have severely impacted.

Let me give a few examples of what could have been done and what should be done. At a time when big banks have nearly $1 trillion in excess reserves parked at the Fed, the Fed has not required these institutions to increase lending to small and medium-sized businesses as a condition of the bailout. In other words, instead of the Fed just giving money to these financial institutions, the Fed should have said: We are giving you this money in order to get it into the economy. Start providing affordable loans to small businesses.

At a time when large corporations are more profitable than ever, the Fed did not demand that corporations that received this backdoor bailout create jobs and expand the economy once they returned to profitability. So what is going on in America? Unemployment is officially at 9.8 percent and the real unemployment rate is 17 percent, but Wall Street is now doing fine.

A few years ago, Wall Street earned some 40 percent of all profits in America, and they are doing great. But what the

Fed should have done and should do now is to tell Wall Street: You are part of the economy. You are not an isolated area just living for yourselves. You have to be a part of the productive economy. You have to lend money to small businesses to start creating jobs.

My office intends to investigate whether these secret Fed loans, in some cases, turned out to be direct corporate welfare to big banks that may have used those loans not to reinvest in the economy but, rather, to lend back to the Federal Government at a higher rate of interest by purchasing Treasury securities. Now, we don't know that. Maybe that is true, maybe it is not true, but we will take a look at it. In other words, did the Fed give one-half of 1 percent loans to a bank and that bank then purchased a Treasury security at 2 or 3 percent? If so, you have a 2 percent profit margin, and that is nothing but corporate welfare. The goal of the bailout was not to make Wall Street richer; the goal was to expand our economy and put people to work.

Furthermore, we know that as part of the TARP agreement, there was an effort to say to the financial institutions: We are not bailing you out in order for you to get huge compensation packages. We are not going to give you Federal money so you can make all kinds of money. We put limitations on executive compensation.

Did the Fed play the role of allowing some of the large financial institutions to pay back the TARP money, use the Fed money, and then continue with their very high executive compensation? We don't know, but it is worth investigating.

Furthermore—and this is an issue I have worked on for a number of years. We know every major religion on Earth—Christianity, Judaism, Islam, you name it—has always felt that usury is immoral. What we mean by usury is that when someone doesn't have a lot of money and you loan them money, you don't get blood out of a stone. You can't ask for outrageously high interest rates when somebody is hurting. That is immoral. Every major religion, all great philosophers have written about this. Yet today we have millions of people in our country—and I hear from Vermonters every week on this issue—who are paying 25 percent or 30 percent and in some cases even higher interest rates on their credit cards—20 percent, 30 percent interest rates. That is getting blood out of a stone. Yet many of the credit card companies were bailed out by the taxpayers of this country. What the Fed must do is say to those companies: Sorry, you can't continue to rip off the American people and charge them 25 percent or 30 percent interest rates.

As it happens, the four largest banks in this country, which are Bank of America, JPMorgan Chase, Wells Fargo, and Citigroup, issue half of all mortgages in this country. Four huge financial institutions issue half of all mortgages in this country. That unto itself is a huge problem. They issue half of all mortgages, two-thirds of all credit cards. That speaks to another issue about the need to start breaking up these financial institutions. But when you have a handful of banks that received huge bailouts from the Federal Government that are issuing two-thirds of the credit cards in this country, it seems to me to be somewhat absurd that the Fed did not say to them: Sorry, you can't charge people 25 or 30 percent interest rates on your credit cards. The same principle applies to mortgages. I don't have to tell anybody in this country that we have seen millions of folks lose their homes through foreclosure, and once again we see that the four largest banks in this country—Bank of America, JPMorgan Chase, Wells Fargo, and Citigroup—issue half of all mortgages. Four banks issue two-thirds of the credit cards and half of the mortgages. We bail these financial institutions out. Don't they have some responsibility to the American people? How many more Americans could have remained in their homes if the Fed had required those bailed-out banks to reduce mortgage payments as a condition of receiving these secret loans?

In terms of the interest rates on credit cards, a lot of people don't know this, but right now the banks are able to charge as much as they want to charge, but, in fact, credit unions are not.

Right now, we are looking at a situation where over one-quarter of all credit cardholders in this country are now paying interest rates above 20 percent and in some cases as high as 79 percent. In my view, when credit card companies charge over 20 percent interest, they are not engaged in the business of making credit available to their customers; they are involved in extortion and loan-sharking—nothing essentially different than gangsters who charge outrageously high prices for their loans and who break kneecaps when their victims can't afford to pay them. So that is where we are right now.

I get calls—and I am sure every other Senator gets calls—from constituents who are very upset. They are going deeper and deeper into debt because they can't pay 25 or 30 percent interest rates on their credit cards. We bailed out the credit card companies. There was no provision that said: Stop ripping off the American people. Stop these companies from committing usury.

We are working on legislation that would say to these private banks not to charge any more money for the credit they provide than do the credit unions. It is going to be a tough fight because the lobbyists from Wall Street are all over this place. Wall Street spends huge amounts of money in campaign contributions, and it is going to be tough. But I think we need to pass that. I think the Fed needs to be much more active, in terms of what kinds of interest rates credit card companies should be paying.

Today, I am going to focus a lot, obviously, on an agreement reached between the President and the Republican leadership, which I think does not serve the American people well. One of the areas, as I mentioned earlier, where I think we could do a lot better in addressing the crisis of high unemployment in this Nation is by investing the kinds of money we need in our infrastructure.

According to the American Society of Civil Engineers, they graded America's roads, public transit, and aviation with a D. They said we must invest $2.2 trillion over the next five years simply to get a passable grade. Unfortunately, in the agreement struck between the President and the Republican leadership, to the best of my knowledge, not one nickel is going into investing in our infrastructure.

Let me tell you why we need to invest in infrastructure. First, that is where you can create the millions of jobs we desperately need in order to get us out of this recession. Second of all, we need to invest in infrastructure because, if we don't, we will become less and less competitive internationally.

According to the National Surface Transportation Policy and Revenue Study Commission, $225 billion is needed annually for the next 50 years to upgrade our surface transportation system to a state of good repair and create a more advanced system. The Federal Highway Administration reports that $130 billion must be invested annually for a 20-year period to improve our bridges and the operational performance of our highways. At present, one in four of the Nation's bridges is either structurally deficient or functionally obsolete. One in four of our bridges is either structurally deficient or functionally obsolete. Yet in this agreement struck by the President and the Republican leadership, to the best of my knowledge, not one nickel is going into our infrastructure. We need to invest in our infrastructure. We need to improve our infrastructure. When we do that, we can create millions of jobs.

The Federal Transit Administration says $22 billion must be invested annually for a 20-year period to improve conditions and performances for our major transit systems. In Vermont, the situation is no different than in the rest of the country. Thirty-five percent of Vermont's 2,700 bridges—

nearly 1,000 bridges—are functionally obsolete. In recent years, we have had to shut down bridges, which caused a lot of inconvenience to people who live in those areas, to workers who had to get to work using a bridge. Nearly half the bridges in Vermont have structural deficiencies. Rural transit options are few and far between, making rural, low-income Vermonters especially vulnerable to spikes in gas prices. In other words, in Vermont, and in other areas of rural America, you have one choice in the vast majority of cases as to how you get to work. That one choice is that you get in your car, you pay $3 for a gallon of gas, and that is it. That is because rural transportation in this country is very weak.

We can create jobs building the buses and vans we need, making it easier and cheaper for workers in rural America to get to work. In urban areas, it is no different. Transit systems in Chicago, New York, and even here in Washington, DC, are in disrepair. Let's improve and repair them. That makes us more efficient, more productive, and more competitive, and it creates jobs now. Not one nickel, as far as I can understand, has been invested in our infrastructure in this agreement.

The United States invests just 2.4 percent of GDP in infrastructure; whereas, Europe invests twice that amount.

Here is something I think every American should be keenly aware of and very worried about. I don't have to tell anybody that the Chinese economy is exploding every single day in almost every way. In China, they are investing almost four times our rate—or 9 percent—of their GDP annually in their infrastructure. Years ago, I was in Shanghai, China. I was coming from the airport to downtown as part of a congressional delegation. While we were on the bus coming in, my wife noticed something. She said: What was that? There was a blur that went by the window. Of course, I didn't notice it; she did. It turned out that blur was an experimental train they were working on—high-speed rail, which is now operational there, and other similar prototypes are being developed in China. Here we are, the United States of America, which for so many years led the world in so many ways, and now you are seeing a newly developing country such as China with high-speed rail all over their country, making them more productive and efficient, and in our cities, our subways are breaking down. Amtrak is going 50, 60 miles an hour, and the Chinese and Europeans have trains going hundreds of miles an hour.

This is the United States of America. Maybe I am old-fashioned. I think we can do it too. I think we can rebuild our rail system, make our country more efficient and create jobs.

China invested $186 billion in rail from 2006 to 2009, and according to the *New York Times*, within two years, they will open 42 new high-speed rail lines, with trains reaching speeds of 200 miles an hour. That is China. So I think if China can do it, the United States of America can do it. That is the way to rebuild America, make us stronger and create jobs.

By 2020, China plans to add 26,000 additional miles of tracks for freight and travel, as well as 230,000 miles of new or improved roads, and 97 new airports—97 new airports. Does anybody in America have the same problem I have when you go to the airport, where you are waiting in line and you have to deal with all the problems of older airports? China is building 97 new ones. We are not. If we are going to be effective in the international economy, and if our kids will have decent jobs, it is high time we woke up and began investing in our infrastructure. So that is not only to improve the long-term strength of America, our economic prowess, but it is also to create jobs right now that we desperately need.

Unfortunately, in this bill, this tax agreement between the President and the Republican leadership, there are many billions of dollars going into tax breaks for corporations. But there is not a whole lot of money—in fact, zero dollars—going into rebuilding our infrastructure.

Similarly—and I know there has been debate forever on this issue. There may be a small breakthrough. I don't have to tell Americans, least of all the people in Vermont, about what happens when the weather gets cold and you are forced to pay very high prices for heating oil. The time is long overdue for us to make the investments we need to transform our energy system away from coal, away from oil. We are spending as a nation—and everybody in America has to appreciate this—$350 billion every single year—$1 billion a day, roughly—importing oil from Saudi Arabia and other foreign countries, in order to make our economy go and in order to keep people warm.

Let me be very clear. The royal family of Saudi Arabia, which is our major source of oil, is doing just fine. Don't worry about the royal family of Saudi Arabia. They have zillions and zillions of dollars. Maybe it is a good idea that we seek energy independence, that we break our dependence on fossil fuel, and become more energy efficient, which, by the way, investing in public transportation certainly will do, and we move to sustainable energy, such as wind, solar, geothermal, and biomass. Guess what. China is doing that. Many of the solar panels coming into this country are not made in the United States but are made in China. They are big into wind turbines. I think the time is now for us to rebuild our infrastructure and create the jobs we desperately need.

Again, unfortunately, despite the enormous infrastructure needs we have in this country, this agreement, signed by the President and the Republican leadership, does not do that. When we talk about transforming our energy system and moving away from fossil fuel and making our homes more energy efficient and building solar panels, moving toward solar thermal power, in the Southwest of this country—New Mexico, Arizona, Nevada—we have some of the best solar exposure in the entire world. There are estimates that just in the Southwest of this country, on Federal land, we can provide 30 percent of the electricity American homes need, if we move toward solar thermal. We need to invest in our transmission lines.

What we are talking about is massive investment to create jobs, make us energy independent, clean up the environment, and deal with the huge amount of greenhouse gas emissions which are contributing to global warming. That is a win-win-win situation. Yet we are not seeing that in this bill.

I wish to tell you something, Mr. President. I will get into this at greater length later. When we talk about our good friends in the oil industry—and I am not here to make a long speech about BP and what they have done in Louisiana, et cetera. I want everybody to know this. I will get into this at greater length later. Last year, our friends at Exxon Mobil—and ExxonMobil has historically been the most profitable corporation in the history of the world. Last year, Exxon Mobil had, for them, a very bad year. They only made $19 billion in profit. Based on $19 billion, you might be surprised to know that Exxon Mobil reported to the SEC that not only did it avoid paying any federal income taxes, they got a $156 million refund from the IRS. How is that? For those of you who are working in an office, working in a factory, earning your $30,000, $40,000, $50,000, $60,000 a year, you pay taxes.

But if you are Exxon Mobil, and you made $19 billion in profits last year, not only did you not pay any federal income taxes in 2009, you got a $156 million refund from the IRS.

It is not just the large oil companies that do not pay their fair share of taxes. I am going to get into this a little bit later, but when we try to understand why we have such a huge national debt and a $1.3 trillion deficit, it is also important to understand that many large and profitable corporations avoid virtually all of their tax responsibility.

In August 2008, the General Accountability Office issued a report. According to this report, two out of every three corporations in the United States paid no Federal income taxes between 1998 and 2005. We have a $13.8 trillion national debt, and according to a GAO report published in August of 2008 two out of every three corporations in the United States paid no Federal income taxes between 1998 and 2005. Amazingly, these corporations had a combined $2.5 trillion in sales but paid no income taxes to the IRS.

Furthermore, according to a report from Citizens For Tax Justice, 82 Fortune 500 companies in America paid zero or less in Federal income taxes in at least one year from 2001 to 2003. That is a report from Citizens For Tax Justice. And the Citizens For Tax Justice report goes on to say:

"In the years they paid no income tax, these companies earned $102 billion in U.S. profits. But instead of paying $35.6 billion in income taxes, as the statutory 35 percent corporate tax rate seems to require, these companies generated so many excess tax breaks that they received outright tax rebate checks from the U.S. Treasury totaling $12.6 billion.

That is from the Citizens For Tax Justice report."

So when we take a comprehensive look at what is going on in this country, why we have a $13.8 trillion national debt, it is terribly important to understand that while the middle class pays its share of taxes, there are many large corporations that not only are paying nothing in federal income taxes, they are getting rebates from the Federal Government.

I will go into greater length later on, but as a member of the Budget Committee I can tell you we discuss quite often how every single year—every single year—corporate interests and wealthy individuals stash away huge amounts of money in tax savings in the Cayman Islands, Bermuda, and other countries in order to avoid paying their taxes in the United States of America. These are American corporations turning their backs on the American people, saying—as Mrs. Helmsley said so many years ago, many of you remember—only the little people pay taxes. Only the working stiffs out there pay taxes.

If you are a large corporation and you have a good lawyer or a good accountant, you know what to do. You invest your money in the Cayman Islands and in Bermuda, and you don't have to pay American taxes. But, by the way, as the Federal Reserve emergency lending disclosure report last week indicated, no problem; you get bailed out. When things get bad, you will be bailed out by the American taxpayers. On and on and on it goes. The rich and large corporations get richer, the CEOs earn huge compensation packages, and when things get bad, don't worry; Uncle Sam and the American taxpayers are here to bail you out. But when you are in trouble, well, we just can't afford to help you, if you are in the working class or the middle class of this country.

I want to return for a moment to the agreement that the President and the Republican leadership negotiated because I think that is the issue that all of America is now talking about. The President and the Republican leadership say it is a good deal. Democrats in the House yesterday said: Wait a second. It doesn't look to us like it is a good deal. In fact, we don't even want to bring it up on the floor of the House. In the Senate, I can tell you there are a number of us—I don't know how many—who say: Wait a minute. This is not a good deal for the middle class, it is not a good deal for our kids, and it is not a good deal for our workers. We can negotiate a better deal. The reason we are trying to delay passage of this agreement—and I hope very much it doesn't have the votes here—is we want the American people to stand and say: Wait a second, it makes no sense to us to be giving huge tax breaks to the richest people in this country—literally millionaires and billionaires—and driving up the national debt so our kids can pay more in taxes in order to pay off that debt.

This is a transfer of wealth. It is Robin Hood in reverse. We are taking from the middle class and working families and we are giving it to the wealthiest people in this country. I believe the agreement struck between the President and the Republican leadership is a bad deal. There are some good parts to it, but, by and large, it is not a good deal. We can do better, and the American people must stand up and work with us. They must get on their phones and call their Senators and call their Congressmen and Congresswomen. They must make their voices heard and say: Enough is enough. The rich have it all right now—the top 1 percent earns 23½ percent of all income, more than the bottom 50 percent— and it is absurd that we continue to bail out people who do not need any help and who are doing just fine.

I am here to take a stand against this bill, and I am going to do everything I can to defeat this bill. I am going to tell my colleagues and the American people exactly why, in my view, this is not good legislation. Let me just tick off some of the reasons I think this bill does not serve the best interests of the disappearing middle class of this country.

I don't know what kind of telephone calls the Presiding Officer is receiving from Colorado, but I can tell you that in the last three days alone, according to my front desk staff both here in Washington and in Vermont, we are over 5,000 telephone calls and e-mails, and I believe well over 98 percent of those messages are against this agreement. I don't know to what degree that is indicative of what is going on all over this country, but I suspect it is not radically different in other states. I think the American people are saying, with a $13.8 trillion national debt, let's not give tax breaks to billionaires and drive up that national debt, forcing our kids to pay more in taxes, and at the same time have Republicans coming forward to start slashing Medicare and Medicaid and Social Security because of this large debt that we are making larger.

I appeal to my conservative friends. I am not a conservative, but many conservatives have spent their entire political careers saying we cannot afford to drive up the national debt, that it is unsustainable. I agree with that. So vote against this agreement because it is driving up the national debt. In a significant way it is doing that by giving tax breaks to people who absolutely don't need it.

Once again, for those people who are earning $1 million a year or more, on average—on average—they will be getting a $100,000-a-year tax break, and for people earning $100 million a year, that number will be a lot higher. Who believes that makes any sense at all?

Let me give some other reasons I think this agreement is a bad agreement. The President says: Well, yes, we are going to extend tax breaks for all, including the top 2 percent. But don't worry, it is only going to be for two years—not to worry, it is only going to be for two years.

Well, maybe that will be the case. But you know what. I doubt that very much. I have been in Congress long enough to know if you extend a tax break, it is very hard to undo that extension because if we can't tell our Republican colleagues that it is absurd to continue giving tax breaks to millionaires and billionaires—if we can't do it now—what makes you think we will do it in the midst of a Presidential election?

I say that as somebody who admires and likes the President. The President is a friend of mine. But his credibility has been severely damaged. If he is going to go forward, and if he is the Democratic nominee, I suspect he will say: Yes, I extended it for two years against my will; but, don't worry, I am going to repeal them after two years. Tell me, who will believe him? His credibility has been severely damaged. We are caving in on this issue and we should not be.

The polls show us the American people do not believe millionaires and billionaires need more tax breaks. If the calls to my office are indicative of what is going on in this country, there is overwhelming opposition to that agreement.

So I am saying that while the President says don't worry, that this is only temporary, I don't like it. But it is only two years. I have my doubts. I expect in two years, if this agreement goes forward, it will be extended again. As you know, Mr. President, they wanted 10 years on this extension of tax breaks for the rich. I have my strong suspicion that is exactly what will happen, if not made permanent. This country cannot afford to give tax breaks to millionaires and billionaires and have the middle class pay higher taxes to pay them off.

I want to say also that while a lot of attention has been focused on the personal income tax issue, that is not the only unfair tax proposal in this agreement. This agreement continues the Bush-era 15 percent tax rate on capital gains and dividends.

Let me be clear about what that means. It means those people who make their living off of their investments—if you invest, if you earn dividends—will continue to pay a substantially lower tax rate than the average American person in the working class, middle class—our firemen, our teachers, our nurses. Those people are not going to pay 15 percent. They pay a higher rate than folks who have capital gains and dividends. I think that is wrong. This agreement extends those provisions.

Furthermore—and this is a point that has to be made over and over—this agreement between the President and the Republicans lowers the estate tax rate to 35 percent and exempts the first $5 million of an estate from taxation. Under this agreement, the estate tax will decline to 35 percent. Under President Clinton, when the economy was much stronger, the estate tax was 55 percent.

Now, I know the Republicans have done a very good job in trying to convince the American people this is a so-called death tax; that in every family in America, when a loved one dies, the family is going to have to pay 35 percent, 45 percent, or 55 percent. I have had people in Burlington, Vermont, come up to me and say: What are you doing? I have $30,000 in the bank that I want to leave to my kids. Why are you forcing my kids to pay such a large tax?

So let me be very clear. The Republicans have done a very good job in totally distorting this issue.

The estate tax is paid only by the top three-tenths of 1 percent of families in America. If you are in the middle class, even if you are modestly wealthy, even if you are wealthy, or if you are poor, if you are lower middle class, you don't pay a nickel in estate tax if somebody in your family were to die and leave you wealth—not a nickel. This applies not just to the rich but to the very, very rich.

What the Republicans have been arguing for several years now is they want to repeal the estate tax entirely. If they were successful in doing that, that would mean increasing the national debt by some $1 trillion over a 10-year period and all of the benefits—not some, all of the benefits—go to the top three-tenths of 1 percent; 99.7 percent of the people do not gain one nickel.

What is in this agreement is not what the Republicans ideally want, which is a repeal of the tax entirely, but what they do get is a reduction to 35 percent with an exemption on the first $5 million of an individual's estate.

Here is a chart which indicates just what I said a moment ago. "Repealing the estate tax would add more than $1 trillion to the deficit over 10 years." It is over $1 trillion, and the beneficiaries of it are just the very wealthy.

Let me give an example of what the repeal of the estate tax would mean. I will read it right off this chart.

Sam Walton's family, the heirs to the Walmart fortune, are worth an estimated $89.6 billion. The Walton family would receive an estimated $32.7 billion tax break if the estate tax was completely repealed.

This is what our Republican friends want.

This agreement between the President and the Republicans certainly does not repeal the estate tax, but it does significantly lower the rates that the richest people, the very richest people in this country, would have to pay.

(Mr. UDALL of Colorado assumed the chair.)

Two days ago, I brought to the floor of the Senate a very simple piece of legislation. I think how that legislation was treated speaks volumes about the debate we are having now. This legislation said that with over 50 million senior citizens on Social Security and disabled vets for the second year in a row not getting a cost-of-living adjustment, a COLA—over 50 million seniors on Social Security and disabled vets not getting any COLA at all—despite the fact their prescription drug costs are going up and their health care costs are going up, they got no COLA. I said I think that in these tough times, it is appropriate that we provide those folks—if we cannot get them a COLA, let's get them the equivalent of a measly 2 percent COLA, a $250 check to all of our seniors and disabled vets. That is what we did, by the way, in the stimulus package. That is all. For over 50 million people, a $250 check costs our government about $14 billion. Yet I could not get one Republican vote in support of that. Republicans say: My goodness, imagine a senior or disabled vet living on $15,000 or $20,000 a year getting a $250 check. What an outrage. We have different priorities, they say. We want to give a $1 million tax break to somebody who earns $50 million a year. That about says it all. If you are very, very rich, the good news is you are going to get more tax breaks. But if you are a senior or disabled vet, we can't get you a $250 check.

I will say that the vote on the floor of the Senate was 53 people in favor of providing that one-time check, 45 against— 53 to 45: We won. But here in the Senate, majority does not rule. Republicans filibuster almost everything, and it requires 60 votes. We did not get the 60 votes, and seniors did not get that check. I am going to do my best to see that they do get it. We are going to bring that issue back again and again.

I raise that issue to tell you that one of the very weakest proposals in this agreement, totally outrageous, is the decrease in taxes for the estate tax.

There is another issue I want to touch on. I am going to spend a lot of time on this issue because it has not gotten the coverage and the attention I think it deserves.

This agreement deals with the so-called payroll tax holiday. I know the Vice President and the President and others have been touting this. They say this is really a good thing because it will put more money into the pockets of the working people. What will happen—right now, if you are a worker, you put 6.2 percent into Social Security. It is going to be reduced for one year to 4.2 percent. You get the difference, and this is really a good thing. All of us want to see working people have more money in their pockets. That is what we do. That is what we are fighting for.

But let me be clear that while on the surface this so-called payroll tax holiday sounds like a good idea for working people, it is actually a very bad idea. What the American people should understand is that this payroll tax holiday originated from rightwing Republicans whose ultimate goal, trust me, is not to put more money into the pockets of working families; it is the ultimate destruction of Social Security. What they understand is that if we divert funding that is supposed to go into the Social Security trust fund, this will ultimately weaken the long-term financial viability of Social Security. In other words, what we are doing is, for the very first time, diverting money which is supposed to go into the Social Security trust fund and we are giving it to workers today. It is like eating our seed.

Rather than going into Social Security, the President says: Don't worry, this is going to be covered this year by the Federal Government. We have never seen that before. I don't want Social Security to be dependent on the Federal Government because the Federal Government has a $13.8 trillion national debt. And what I worry about is this is not just a one-year provision; this also could be extended.

Let me quote Barbara Kennelly.

I am glad to see I am joined here on the floor by one of the strongest fighters for working families in the Senate, Senator *Sherrod Brown* of Ohio. I just want to say this before I ask him a question or before he asks me a question or whatever the protocol is.

I want to quote what Barbara Kennelly, the president and CEO of the National Committee to Preserve Social Security and Medicare, said. This is one of the largest senior citizens groups in America.

"Even though Social Security contributed nothing to the current economic crisis, it has been bartered in a deal that provides deficit-busting tax cuts for the wealthy."

Here is the key point:

"Diverting $120 billion in Social Security contributions for a so-called 'tax holiday' may sound like a good deal for workers now, but it's bad business for a program that a majority of middle-class seniors will rely upon in the future."

Barbara Kennelly, president and CEO of the National Committee to Preserve Social Security and Medicare.

I am joined by my very good friend from Ohio, and I want to ask him his sense of this overall agreement.

Mr. BROWN of Ohio. My sense is similar to yours. I was just on a TV show a minute ago. I was asked, the liberals or the conservatives, what they think about this. This really is not a liberal-conservative issue. First of all, the tax cuts overwhelmingly go to the wealthiest taxpayers. We are seeing the kinds of tax cuts that millionaires and billionaires get from the income tax and from the estate tax. But it is also equally important that it blows a hole in our budget deficit.

In some sense, we are borrowing tens of billions of dollars every year now—if this agreement becomes law, we are borrowing tens of billions of dollars every year from the Chinese, and we are putting it on the credit cards of our children and grandchildren for them to pay off who knows when, and then we are giving these tax cuts to millionaires and billionaires. In those simple terms, it doesn't make sense. It doesn't make sense in our relationship with China. It doesn't make sense in the lost jobs that come from that China trade policy. It doesn't make sense in undermining the middle class. It doesn't make sense in terms of fairness in the tax system. It doesn't make sense for our children and grandchildren and the burden they are going to have to bear to pay off this debt. Giving a millionaire a tax cut and charging it to our kids, who are paying taxes on, unfortunately, in the last few years, declining wages, is morally reprehensible.

I know Senator *Sanders* has been on the floor two hours now talking about this and how important it is and really analyzing it and educating about it and all that. I think about the economic policy, too, that this embodies.

Nine or 10 years ago, Senator *Sanders* and the Presiding Officer, when he was a Member of the House, Senator *Udall* from Colorado, and I and others voted against the Bush tax cuts of 2001 and 2003, principally because those tax cuts overwhelmingly went to the wealthy and ended up adding to our national debt. We had a surplus then. We sure don't now. We had the largest surplus we ever had in 2001. It blew a hole in that. But we passed those tax cuts under the belief, those who supported it—President Bush and Senator Mc-Connell and so many others—under the belief that that kind of trickle-down economics would grow our economy.

In the eight years—and this is not partisan, this is not opinion, this is fact—from January 1, 2001, to January 1, 2009, President Bush's eight years, we actually had private sector job loss in this country. Contrast that with a different economic policy—January 1, 1993, to January 1, 2001, the Clinton eight years. Again, this isn't partisan, this isn't opinion, this is fact. During the Clinton eight years, we had 21 million private sector jobs created—21 million private sector jobs created—and literally zero private sector jobs in the Bush eight years of trickle-down economics.

Why would we blow a hole in the budget, which this bill does, for our kids to pay off? Why would we continue an economic policy that clearly did not work for this country? It didn't work for the middle class. We saw middle-class wages—not only no job increase during those eight years, except for the people at the very top, we saw actual wage stagnation or worse. Most Americans did not get a raise during the eight Bush years. Most Americans simply saw their wages flat or in many cases decline. The superwealthy saw a big increase in their incomes and in their net assets. And now we are going to give a tax break to them.

This is not class warfare. Lots of people I know have a lot of money. I don't have any ill will for them. But why would we help those people who have done so very well and then have our children pay for it?

Senator *Sanders* just mentioned the letter from Barbara Kennelly from one of the largest seniors' organizations in the country and what this will mean for Social Security. Here is my fear. If this is passed, we are going to see our budget deficit increase, according to the Congressional Budget Office, about $900 billion because of this package, $800-some billion over the next couple of years.

As soon as it is signed by President Obama, even though it was negotiated with the Republican Senate leadership and overwhelming numbers of Republicans in the Senate and House—I assume they are going to vote for it—they are going to say: Look at the huge budget deficit President Obama created. From that day on, they are going to go after ways to cut the budget. That is OK. I agree we need to deal with spending and taxes and the whole picture.

But I also know from watching Republicans—I saw them in the House when they moved toward Medicare privatization in 2003, 2004, and 2005. They had some success. Fortunately, we were able to beat back most of it. I remember that in 2005, after President Bush was reelected in a very close race, he spoke repeatedly about privatizing Social Security. I know that is what they want to do. In the 1990s, Speaker Gingrich—fortunately beaten back by President Clinton—tried to privatize Medicare.

That is the way they cut the budget, they go after Medicare and Social Security. So this vote on this package—to me, we need to call the President, write the President, work with the President to say: No deal, and this has to be something very different from what it is now because it will cause huge deficits our children and grandchildren will have to bear. It will not help the economy appreciably because we saw what the trickle-down economic policies of the Bush years did. It does not help the middle class enough.

So it is pretty clear to me how this jeopardizes Social Security, how it jeopardizes Medicare, how it will force more cuts and more pressure on those programs that have lifted so many people into the middle class. In 1965, when Medicare was first passed, half of the senior citizens in this country had no health insurance—half of the seniors had no health insurance. Today 99 percent of seniors have health insurance, something like that.

I know we are a country now that has created a strong middle class. We have seen that middle class—because of these tax cuts for the wealthy, trickle-down kind of economic policy, we have seen the middle class shrink in the last few years. I do not want that to keep happening. That is why I am very concerned about this. That is why I am working with the Senate to say: No deal. We need to much more seriously focus on not running up a huge debt, on making sure Social Security is protected, on an economic policy that works for the middle class, on a tax policy that is fair to the middle class.

That is why Senator *Sanders'* work is so important on the floor today, taking the floor for a longer period than anybody

I have seen since I have been in the Senate, in a filibuster kind of setting, where he is raising these questions, asking these questions, educating the public, talking to people all over the country, in this Chamber and outside to change this policy.

Mr. SANDERS. If I could interrupt my friend from Ohio and ask him a question, it is on an issue the Senator dealt with last night. Talk about the kind of priorities we have seen in the Senate recently, where just a couple of days ago the Senator and I worked very hard to try to make sure seniors on Social Security and disabled vets were able to get a $250 check at a cost of $14 billion, we could not get one Republican vote for that, while at the same time Republicans are pushing tax breaks of over $1 million a year for the richest people in this country. Does that seem—

Mr. BROWN of Ohio. It tells a story. I came to the floor right after that vote. I had supported it all along. I cosponsored Senator *Sanders'* effort to bring that to the floor, for the $250 check for all seniors and all disabled veterans, I might add, not just Social Security beneficiaries. But I came to the floor right afterwards because I was pretty amazed.

I know there is partisanship here. I know some people think their whole view of the world is to give tax cuts to the richest people of the world and it will all trickle down and we will all do better, it will lift all boats. That is a pretty good economic theory you might have learned at Harvard or you might have learned at Johns Hopkins near here or wherever.

But it does not work. It is a nice theory, but it does not work to lift all boats.

So Senator *Sanders'* effort was to provide a $250 check, one time, at a cost of $14 billion. But one time, not continued $14 billion—one time for seniors who had not had a cost-of-living adjustment in two years. It just seemed to make so much sense when the average senior in this country gets about a $14,000-a-year Social Security check. I think that is about $1,200 a month. That is not their entire income for most seniors, but it is a big part of it. Many seniors live only on that. Many more seniors live on that, but only another couple $300, $400 a month.

There is not inflation maybe for people my age so much in this country, but if you are older and you have a lot of health care costs, there is inflation because the health care costs seem to go up higher than maybe anything but higher education, and maybe as much as that. So it was important that $250 be provided, we think, to every senior in the country and every disabled vet.

What was so amazing about it was that 42 Republican Senators signed a letter saying they would do nothing, nothing in the Senate, until tax cuts for the rich were approved, until they were signed into law.

Now, I have never seen Senators engage in a work stoppage or a strike. I mean, it was not quite a strike, which it is probably illegal for us to strike. I do not know, maybe. But it was a work stoppage.

They are saying: We are not doing anything until you give tax cuts to my rich friends, and I might say also to many people in the House and Senate whose income is in that bracket too. I am not accusing them of that, to be sure, but they were there for their rich friends and their biggest contributors and the wealthiest people in this country. But they were not there for a senior citizen living on $1,200 a month that could use that extra $250.

I have met too many seniors, and I know the Presiding Officer, when he travels to Colorado Springs or he goes to Cimarron or he goes to Denver, I know he hears seniors say: I cut my pills in half because I need my prescription to run for two months rather than one because I cannot afford it. Or I skipped my medicine today because my house is too cold, and I do not have enough heat. We know seniors make those choices. We make choices here, and the choice we made is 42 Republicans made it and blocked it because we need 60 votes. We had a majority of voters, an easy majority, for Senator *Sanders'* effort, 53 votes, 53 votes to do this, the $250, but we need 60 votes.

So 42 Republican Senators engaged in their work stoppage saying: We are not doing anything until we get these tax cuts for the rich. They said no to seniors. I am amazed by that, the callousness. I guess I am even more amazed when you consider—what is today, the 10th—when you consider in two weeks it is Christmas Day. That does not seem to bother them. It does not seem to bother them on unemployment benefits. And 85,000 Ohioans, a week and a half ago, lost their unemployment benefits—85,000. Their holiday season is ruined.

But I guess all of us will go home. I want to go home and be with Connie and my kids on Christmas. My children are grown. We have one grandchild. I want to be with him for as much of Christmas as I can. But we have a job to do today, this week and next week and this month and this year; and that is to extend unemployment benefits to people who have lost them, who are looking for jobs as hard as they can in a great majority of cases, and extending the tax cuts for the middle class and doing the right thing. So far, we have not done that.

I need to go to the airport. But I want to yield back to Senator *Sanders* for his work today. I hope next week, when we come back on Monday, we are prepared to do whatever it takes to say no deal on this one and to make this work for the middle class, make it work for Social Security beneficiaries, make it work for unemployed workers.

Mr. SANDERS. I thank my good friend from Ohio, one of the real fighters for working families in the Senate, not only for coming down here but for his years of efforts. But he makes a very important point. We have a job to do and the job is—I know some people do not believe it. It is a rather radical concept. But our job is to represent working families, the middle class, and not the wealthiest people in this country.

I have four kids, six grandchildren. I look forward to spending the holidays with them. But you know what. We have a job to do, and if it means staying here through Christmas Eve, through New Year's, that is our job. And let's pass a proposal that works well for ordinary families and not just for the wealthiest people in this country.

I wanted to thank Senator *Sherrod Brown* for coming down.

What I want to say now is, when you look at this agreement, we have talked now about the absurdity, in the middle of a time when we have a $13.8 trillion national debt, of giving tax breaks to people who do not need it. Senator *Brown* and I have talked about the dangers inherent in this payroll tax holiday and what it might mean for the future of Social Security. But I also wanted to make another point; that is, that there are many billions of dollars in this proposal going to a variety of business tax cuts. Some of them, in fact, might work; some of them, in fact, might not work. But what is very clear is, if your goal is to create as many jobs as possible for every dollar of investment, this particular approach is not very effective.

When we talk about tax breaks for corporations and companies, what we should be aware of is that corporate America today—today—is sitting on close to $2 trillion in cash. They have that cash on hand. The problem is not that they do not have the money, the problem is that working people do not have the money to buy the products these guys are producing. I believe, and not just me but I think a variety of economists from across the board, it makes a lot more sense if we are serious about creating jobs to invest in our infrastructure.

I say that for a number of reasons. When you put money into roads and bridges and public transportation, you are creating, for every dollar you spend, far more jobs than giving a variety of tax breaks. That is an economic fact.

Second of all, when you are investing in our infrastructure, not only are you creating jobs short term, you are leaving the country with long-term improvement that increases our competitiveness in a very tough global economy. I mentioned a moment ago, and we will get back to it later, China is investing huge amounts of money into high-speed rail, into their roads, into their bridges. Yet if you drive around certain parts of America, you think we are a Third World nation. You have roads with all kinds of potholes. You have bridges which you cannot go across. You have rail systems where trains are going slower—there is a study out there that I am going to get to later—where somebody said that decades and decades ago, it took less time to go from various parts of this country to the other on trains than it does today because our rail beds are in such bad shape.

So if we are going to make our country competitive, we have to invest in infrastructure. It creates jobs. It adds long-term value to this country. Unfortunately, in this agreement, there is, to the best of my knowledge, not one nickel going into infrastructure. It is important that we, in fact, add provisions which do invest in our infrastructure and create jobs.

Another point that should be made when we look at this so-called compromise agreement established by the President and the Republican leadership is that in the agreement there is an extension of unemployment benefits for 13 months. Now, there is zero question, in my mind; that is something that absolutely has to be done. Right now—Senator *Brown* made this point—we have millions of Americans who have, through no fault of their own, lost their jobs. Maybe their plants went to China. Maybe their companies could not get the loans they needed to stay in business. Small businesses are going under, big businesses are shutting plants. No question we have to extend unemployment benefits.

But what bothers me is that this provision in this agreement, which is a good provision, suggests that this is a hard-won compromise; that the Republicans conceded something and they agreed to a 13-month extension of unemployment benefits. But here is the fact. The fact is, for the last 40 years, when unemployment rates have gone above 7.2 percent, Republicans and Democrats, in a nonpartisan way, have come together to say, of course, we are going to extend unemployment. This is America. We are not going to let working families who are suffering hard times because, through no fault of their own, they have lost their jobs, we are not going to let them lose their homes or not enable them to feed their families. This is America. We are not going to do that.

Republicans have said that for 40 years. Democrats have said that for 40 years. Democratic and Republican Presidents, leaders in the House and Senate, have said that. So to say: Oh, my goodness, the Republicans made a major concession; they are going to allow the extension of unemployment benefits for 13 months, that is not a concession. That has been bipartisan public policy for the last 40 years.

Now, I have been expressing to you and to the American people why I think this is not a good agreement, why I think this agreement should be defeated and why I believe we can put together a much better agreement.

I do want to be clear. There are positive aspects to this agreement which should be maintained in an improved proposal. Let me mention some of them. This proposal, in addition to extending unemployment benefits for 13 months, extends the middle-class tax cuts. That is obviously something we have to do. The reality is that the middle class is collapsing. During the Bush years we saw a $2,200 decline in median family income. Working families are hurting. There is no question. To not extend that tax cut for 98 percent of America would be a travesty. So we have to maintain those tax cuts, and that is a positive thing in the agreement which obviously any future agreement must maintain.

Also in this agreement is the earned-income tax credit for working Americans, a very important provision, and the child and college tax credits are also in this agreement. These proposals will keep millions of Americans from slipping out of the middle class and into poverty, and they will allow millions of Americans to send their kids to college. I am not here to say to the President or the Vice President that there are not any good proposals and parts of this agreement. There are. But we can do much better.

What the President says—and he makes a valid point— show me the votes; he is good at counting. We tried a proposal here, where we only got 53 votes, which said we are going to extend the tax breaks for the middle class and not the very rich. The President knows, as everybody else knows, that around here Republicans filibuster everything. We need 60 votes, and he said: Show me the votes. This is what I would say: What our job right now is about is reaching out to the American people from one end of the country to the other, from California to Vermont, including a lot of our very conservative states. Frankly, it is not a conservative approach to substantially increase the national debt by giving tax breaks to billionaires. How many times have we been here on the floor hearing our Republican colleagues give long speeches about the danger and the unsustainability of a $13.8 trillion national debt and a $1.3 trillion deficit? We have heard it day after day. That is their mantra. If they believe that, why are they voting for a proposal that substantially increases the national debt for the very unproductive reason of giving tax breaks to the richest people who don't need it?

The reason we have to defeat this proposal and fight for a much better one is, I would hope that people throughout this country, from Vermont and Colorado, and many of our conservative states, would come forward and say: Wait a second. I do not want to see my kids and grandchildren pay more in taxes because we have borrowed money from China to increase the national debt in order to give tax breaks to millionaires and billionaires who have done extraordinarily well in recent years and, by the way, have seen a significant decline in their effective tax rate.

I know the Chair has heard wealthy people such as Warren Buffett make the point over and over again that what he really pays in taxes, his effective tax rate, is lower than his secretary's. All over this country we have examples where very rich people are able to stash money in the Cayman Islands, take advantage of all types of loopholes, and are paying rather low effective tax rates, in many cases lower than police officers or firemen or teachers or nurses. Opposition to this agreement should be tripartisan. We should have conservative Republicans, liberal Democrats.

I am an independent progressive. I can tell my colleagues in the last three days my office has received probably close to 3,000 phone calls, 98 percent of them against this agreement, probably higher than 98 percent, and a huge number of e-mails also overwhelmingly against this agreement. I suspect—I don't know it for a fact—that this is the kind of message the American people are sending us all over America. But they have to continue to do so. They have to make it clear so we can win over at least a handful of Republicans and some wavering Democrats and say: Wait a second. We are not going to hold hostage extending middle-class tax breaks in order to give tax breaks to billionaires. We will not hold hostage extending unemployment for workers who have lost their jobs by giving tax breaks to people who don't need it.

If the American people give voice to what they are feeling, that this is not a good agreement, that we can do a lot better, I think we can defeat this proposal, and we can come back with a much better proposal which protects the unemployed, extends unemployment benefits, protects the middle class, extends tax cuts for 98 percent of the working population, and protects a lot of important programs, making college more affordable, making childcare more affordable, and helping us transform our energy system.

There is a lot we can do if we defeat this proposal. We are not going to do it inside the Beltway. Republicans are very united. But what we have to do is win at least a handful of them and some wavering Democrats to say: Mr. President, Republican leadership, you guys have to involve Congress in this discussion.

I was pleased yesterday that the House Democratic caucus said: Sorry, we are not bringing that proposal onto the floor. I applaud Speaker *Pelosi* and the Democratic caucus for saying so. That took courage. Congressman *Welch* from the State of Vermont played an important role. Congressman *Peter DeFazio* played an important role. I congratulate him. I congratulate the caucus for saying we can do better than we are doing.

Let me be frank: We are not going to do better unless the American people stand up and help us. We are going to need a lot of phone calls, a lot of e-mails, a lot of messages so that all of our colleagues in the House and Senate understand the American people do not want to see their kids having to pay off the debt incurred by giving tax breaks to billionaires.

This agreement doesn't come out of the blue. It comes within a context that frightens many people. Many Americans have a sinking feeling that there is something very wrong in our country today. I know my father came to this country at the age of 17 without a penny in his pocket. He became the proudest American one could ever see. He didn't have much of an education, but he knew this country gave him a great opportunity. That is the American story. That is what it is all about. To millions and millions of families, whether they came from other countries, whether they just made it on their own—I know we have heard the Majority Leader *Harry Reid* talking about his experience growing up in a desperately poor family—that is what America is about. But there are a lot of folks out there who believe there is something wrong, and the facts back them up.

What is going on in this country is the middle class is collapsing. Poverty is increasing. I have four kids and six grandchildren. I am not worried about me, but I am worried about what happens to my kids and my grandchildren. We have some wonderful young pages here, and we worry about their futures as well. We don't want to see our kids and grandchildren be the first generation in the modern history of America to have a lower standard of living than their parents. We don't want to see this country's economy move in the wrong way. We don't want a race to the bottom. We want to see our kids live healthier and better lives than we do, not have to work longer hours, not getting a lower quality of education or less education. That is not the history of this great country.

I want to talk about one aspect of what is going on that does not get the kind of attention it deserves. There are obvious reasons why, having to do with who owns the media and corporate control of the media, having to do with who provides the campaign contributions that elect Members of the House and Senate, having to do with all the lobbyists who surround this institution. Wall Street and the oil companies spend hundreds of millions of dollars on campaign contributions. The issue I wish to discuss is who is winning and who is losing in this economy. I come from New England. Everybody follows the Celtics. We follow the Red Sox, the Patriots. What everyone asks is, who won the game? Did the Patriots win or lose? That is what we want to know.

In fact, in America, it is pretty clear in the economy who is winning and losing. The vast majority of people, working people, middle-class people, low-income people are losing. That is who is losing. It is clear who is winning. The wealthiest people are doing phenomenally well. They are winning the economic struggle.

In America today—we don't talk about this too much, but it is time we did—we have the most unequal distribution of wealth and income in the industrialized world. I haven't heard too many people talk about that issue. Why not? Our Republican colleagues want huge tax breaks for the richest people, but the reality is the top 1 percent already today owns more wealth than the bottom 90 percent. How much more do they want? When is enough enough? Do they want it all? We already have millions of families today who have zero wealth. They owe more than they own. Millions of families have below zero wealth. We are living in a situation where the top 1 percent owns more wealth than the bottom 90 percent. The top 1 percent owns more wealth than the bottom 90 percent. That is simply unacceptable.

This is something we must be absolutely ashamed about and have to address, instead of giving tax breaks to billionaires. Maybe we should appreciate the fact that about 25 percent of our children are dependent on food stamps. We should understand that in the industrialized world, the United States, as this chart shows, has the highest rate of childhood poverty. Is this America? Is this America? The United States today has over 20 percent of its kids living in poverty. In Finland, the number is about 2.8 percent; Norway, 3.4 percent; Sweden, maybe 4.2 percent; Switzerland, 6.8 percent. But here we are. If people are watching on television, what they are seeing is the red line. Here is the United States, well over 20 percent. Here is the Netherlands in second place at 9.8 percent. This is the future of America. So we are sitting here talking about an agreement which says: Let's give huge tax breaks to billionaires. And here is the reality. We have a rate of childhood poverty far surpassing any other major country on Earth.

This is the other half of the equation. What do my colleagues think happens when we have millions of kids living in poverty? What do my colleagues think happens when we have kids who are dropping out of school when they are 13 or 14? I talked to a fellow in Vermont who runs one of our jails. He said about half the kids who drop out of school end up in the penal system. That is what happens. The result is, the highest rate of childhood poverty in the industrialized world, and then what we end up with is more people behind bars than any other country on Earth.

China is a Communist totalitarian society, much larger than the United States, which is a democratic society. We have more people in jail than China and more people in jail than any other country. So what we end up doing, which seems to be not terribly bright, is spending perhaps $50,000 a year keeping people in jail because they dropped out of school. They never found a job. They got hooked on drugs or whatever. We pay to put them in jail rather than investing in childcare, in education, in sustaining their families.

So when we look at the context in which this agreement was reached, we have to see that it takes place at a time when the rich are already doing phenomenally well, while we have the highest rate of childhood poverty in the industrialized world.

During the eight years of President Bush, the wealthiest 400 Americans—that is not a lot of people, 400 families—saw their income more than double while their income tax rates dropped almost in half from 1995 to 2007. So you have 400 families—all of whom are already multi-multimillionaires—where during the eight years of President Bush their income more than doubled while their income tax rates dropped almost in half from 1995 to 2007.

I would say to my colleagues in the Senate, we do not have to worry about these guys. They are doing just fine.

They do not need an extension of tax breaks. The wealthiest 400 Americans now earn, on average, $345 million a year, and they pay an effective tax rate of 16.6 percent. How is that? All right. The top 400 wealthiest people in this country earn $345 million a year, and they pay an effective tax rate of 16.6 percent. They do not need an extension of tax breaks.

By the way, for the United States of America, this effective tax rate of 16.6 percent, on average, is the lowest tax rate for the very rich in America that there has ever been on record. So we have already given the wealthiest people in this country the lowest effective tax rates in the history of our country, at least since they have been keeping records. That is what we have done. So the idea of giving these guys—who are doing phenomenally well, who already own more wealth than the bottom 90 percent—more tax breaks is totally absurd.

Under the eight years of President Bush, the wealthiest 400 Americans—we talked about how they doubled their incomes; income is what happens in one year—under the eight years of President Bush, the wealthiest 400 Americans increased their wealth by more than $380 billion. Four hundred families increased their wealth by $380 billion. That averages to almost $1 billion a family. Mr. President, $1 billion in eight years. That is the average; some, obviously, more.

Collectively—I know this is not an issue we talk about too much—the 400 richest Americans have accumulated $1.27 trillion in wealth. If any of them die this year, their heirs can receive, right now, all of this money tax free because the inheritance tax has been eliminated in 2010 as part of the Bush estate tax repeal this year.

Last year, the top 25 hedge fund managers made a combined $25 billion in income—$1 billion per person. OK. So if you are a hedge fund manager, you are doing pretty good. I mentioned a moment ago that we tried just the other day to get checks of $250 out for disabled vets and senior citizens on Social Security who have not had a COLA in two years. We could not get them that check. But last year the top 25 hedge fund managers made a combined $25 billion in income—$1 billion per person. And our Republican friends say: Oh, my word, my word, we have to lower their taxes. Last year, Exxon Mobil, Bank of America, and other large profitable corporations reported to the SEC that they paid no federal income taxes.

So what you have is a federal income tax system which is totally distorted in the sense that it allows large profitable corporations to pay, in some cases—in many cases—zero. In fact, last year—it would be funny if it really was not pathetic—as I understand it, Exxon Mobil, which made $19 billion, reported to the SEC that they paid no federal income taxes. Bank of America—Bank of America got a huge bailout from the American taxpayer, paying their executives all kinds of fancy, huge compensation packages—got a refund check from the IRS according to their SEC filings. That is how absurd the situation is. And people say: Oh, my word, in order to deal with our deficit, we are going to have to cut back on Medicare and Medicaid and education. We cannot afford it. I guess we can afford to allow Exxon Mobil, the most profitable corporation in the history of the world, to make huge sums of money and, according to their annual report, pay nothing in federal income taxes. We can afford to do that, but we cannot afford to protect working families and the middle class.

In the year 2005, one out of every four large corporations in the United States paid no Federal income tax on revenue of $1.1 trillion. Now, what do you think? Maybe before we start cutting Social Security and Medicare and Medicaid and veterans programs, we would want to ask some of these very large and profitable corporations to pay at least something in taxes? From 1998 to 2005, two out of every three corporations in the United States paid no Federal income taxes, according to the GAO.

Sadly, the economic pain millions of people are experiencing did not even begin as a result of the Wall Street bailout. The middle class was collapsing long before that. It is wrong to blame Bush for all the problems. He contributed a lot to it but not all of it. That trend has been going on for many years.

As the *Washington Post* reported last January—let me quote from an article because, again, I want to put the economic reality facing the middle class in contrast to the economic reality facing the very rich in the broad context of this agreement signed by the President and the Republican leadership. As the *Washington Post* reported on January 2, 2010:

"The past decade was the worst for the U.S. economy in modern times. . . ."

"It was, according to a wide range of data, a lost decade for American workers."

"A lost decade for American workers." Do you know why people are furious? Do you know why they are angry at Washington and everybody else? The last decade was, according to the *Washington Post*, a lost decade for American workers.

"There has been zero net job creation since December 1999."

Twelve years of zero job creation, which is why unemployment is so high, not only for the general population but even worse for our young people, kids getting out of high school, young people graduating college.

According to the *Washington Post*—this came from the *Washington Post* in January:

"Middle-income households made less in 2008, when adjusted for inflation, than they did in 1999. . . ."

In other words, the American economy has turned into a nightmare for tens of millions of families. Imagine that.

"Middle-income households made less in 2008, when adjusted for inflation, than they did in 1999—and the number is sure to have declined further during a difficult 2009."

They did not have those numbers, but because of the Wall Street collapse, that certainly is the case.

So what are we talking about? We are talking about, as I have just demonstrated, the people on top seeing a doubling of their income, while their effective tax rates are going down. You are seeing the middle class collapsing.

What this agreement says is that we are going to provide huge tax breaks for millionaires and billionaires. That is insane. Only within the Beltway could an agreement such as that be negotiated.

As I mentioned earlier, in the last three days, we have received thousands and thousands and thousands of phone calls and e-mails to my office, and over 98 percent—I daresay 99 percent—say this is not a good agreement, do not support it.

Mr. President, I have been joined on the floor by the very distinguished Senator from the State of Louisiana. I ask unanimous consent that I be permitted to enter into a colloquy with Senator *Landrieu*.

The PRESIDING OFFICER. Is there objection?

Without objection, it is so ordered.

Mr. SANDERS. I thank Senator *Landrieu* very much for joining us here. I wondered if the Senator could give the American people her thoughts about this agreement and what has been going on.

Ms. LANDRIEU. Mr. President, I thank the Senator from Vermont for his eloquent and passionate presentation for hours this morning. He clearly has presented to this Chamber and to the American people some stark realities that are unpleasant. Some people might even find them hard to believe. But he has done his homework. He has documented what he said. In that backdrop, it does make this agreement, made between the Republican leadership and the President of the United States, even harder for some of us to understand.

I want to acknowledge, as the Senator said—I know there are pressures on all sides, and time is running out; we have to make a decision about tax cuts in a short period of time. We do not have the benefit of several months or even half a year. I understand the pressures of time. But as the Senator from Vermont pointed out, how about the pressures on the middle class? What about these pressures? What about this pain?

I was wondering, because I wanted to ask the Senator from Vermont—I was not able to follow his entire presentation this morning—did he quote from the report "Income Inequality and the Great Recession," done by the U.S. Congress Joint Economic Committee, led by *Charles Schumer*? I ask the Senator, did you quote from this report?

Mr. SANDERS. We quoted from a number of studies, but not that one, I say to the Senator.

Ms. LANDRIEU. I would like to add in our colloquy, if the Senator is aware, according to this report that just came out in September of this year:

"Income inequality has skyrocketed. Economists concur that income inequality has risen dramatically over the past three decades."

Middle-class incomes stagnated under President Bush. During the recovery of the 1990s under President Clinton, middle-class incomes grew at a healthy pace. However, during the jobless recovery of the 2000s under President Bush, that trend reversed course. Middle-class incomes continued to fall well into the recovery, and never regained their 2001 high.

The report goes on to say—which is frightening, which is why I have been raising my voice in opposition so strongly to some parts of this package—high levels of income inequality may precipitate economic crises.

In other words, if the middle class cannot see light at the end of the tunnel and if the economy itself cannot grasp a way for the middle class to grow, I say to the Senator, this recession may never end no matter how much money you give to the very wealthy.

This is the reality we are facing at this moment—how to end this recession.

Republicans weren't completely to blame for it, Democrats weren't completely innocent, or vice versa. It is not about who to blame, it is about how to fix it. We are about to pick up a $980 billion hammer next week in an attempt to fix it. Are we hitting the nail right? We don't have many $980 billion hammers to pick up. We are borrowing this one. So let's get it right. This is an important issue before our country. I think that is what the Senator is saying.

Am I putting words into the Senator's mouth? Is this what the Senator is trying to explain?

Mr. SANDERS. Exactly. The point cannot be overstated. What Senator *Landrieu* is saying is that if you have a collapsing middle class and people are unable to purchase anything, it impacts the entire economy. The economy can't grow. We can't grow jobs if people don't have enough money to buy products made by other people. If all or a substantial part of the wealth in this Nation accrues in the hands of a few, they get three yachts and eight airplanes, I guess, but there is a limit to what they can purchase.

Ms. LANDRIEU. And there is a limit to what they can consume.

What the Senator from Vermont is saying and what I am saying—I want to be very clear, because the Senator and I don't agree on every piece of legislation. He tends to be a little bit more liberal and progressive in his politics than I am, but on this subject we are both equally concerned about the shrinking of the middle class. From my perspective—the Senator may have a different view—I am talking about the broad middle class: incomes of $50,000 to $500,000. In my state, $500,000 of income—not net worth but income—is a huge amount of money. In fact, I brought a graph to show that 84 percent of the households in Louisiana—when I talk about middle class—84 percent of the households in Louisiana make less than $75,000. I said 84 percent. Most people in Louisiana—most—believe they are in the middle class, but 84 percent make below $75,000.

So when I use the term middle class—and we all have a different view—I am saying the broad middle class with incomes between $50,000 and $500,000. If you have $500,000 in income, you are quite wealthy in Louisiana, but I realize we are not New York, Connecticut, or California. Maybe if you make $500,000 or $400,000 in some of these places, you don't consider yourself very wealthy or rich. I think by Louisiana standards you would be, but this is a big nation. So I want to be as broad as I can possibly be here. I am not talking about the wealthy being $400,000 or $500,000. That may not be the case in California. But what we are talking about in this tax bill is borrowing $50 billion to give tax breaks to families earning over $1 million. So as the Senator from Vermont said, whether you put your mark at $250,000 or $500,000—we can disagree about how broad the middle class is, but is there anyone—anyone—anyone in this Chamber on either side of the aisle from any state who believes seriously, giving what the Senator from Vermont just outlined—which is really not debatable; these economic studies are not just from one side of the aisle or another—that we should actually next week provide $50 billion in extended benefits for the families in America who are making more than $1 million a year? Should we do that when the inequities are so great, when the needs of the middle class are so great, when there is no evidence to suggest from any I have seen that is convincing that even after this tax cut the recession will end? We are doing this for two years. What happens if the recession doesn't end and we have borrowed all of this money to provide the extension of these tax cuts, as well as giving $50 billion to the $1 million earners in this country? What do we do then? Go borrow another trillion and try it again? I think we have to try something different.

I don't know if the Senator has another point before I go into a few thoughts.

Mr. SANDERS. Let me ask the Senator—and I thank her very much and I agree with what she has been saying. I was mentioning earlier the calls coming in and the e-mails coming into my office are overwhelming: 99 percent against this. Are you getting similar calls?

Ms. LANDRIEU. I am getting calls, and I am getting about 50 percent for and 50 percent against. The State of Louisiana is a little different than the State of Vermont. Many of the calls coming in from around the country are against giving— well, actually, let me say this: Most of the calls coming in are absolutely against giving tax cuts to people earning over $1 million.

Mr. SANDERS. That is what I am talking about.

Ms. LANDRIEU. Overwhelmingly, people are calling in and saying, Is that really happening? In fact, my office told me today that actually 10 people called who had incomes over $1 million, which I found very interesting, to say they supported my position: Tell Senator *Landrieu* I make $1 million a year and I agree with her. So I know people are listening. I thank those callers.

They make $1 million every year and they said, Please, use the money for somebody else or something else. I am doing fine. I am counting my blessings. I survived the recession. They know that 33,000 people are getting ready to run out of unemployment benefits in Louisiana alone if we don't extend it. They know middle-class families making over $75,000 in income or $200,000 in income or even $500,000—you can have $300,000 of income in Louisiana and be a strong business person and doing very well, and have eight children. The Presiding Officer has large families out in the West. We have very large families in the South. No one ever gives us credit enough, I think, for that. People work very hard, a mother and a father. Their income might be $200,000, $250,000, but with six children, that doesn't go that far these days. I grew up in a neighborhood where we routinely had 12 children in a house. How much money do you think you have to make to feed and clothe and send to college 12 children? My father sent nine of us to college. We never made anywhere near that money. I still think it was a miracle any of us ever got there.

But, nonetheless, the issue is next week we are going to debate this agreement. I wish to say I support extending tax cuts to the middle class, to the broad middle class. But there is something terribly wrong here in Denmark. Something is not right in Denmark if we are spending or borrowing $50 billion, which is about what it costs to extend income tax rates, the lower rate and the dividend rates, and the capital gains rates to people making over $1 million.

Someone on the radio today said, Well, Senator, don't you think giving tax cuts will stimulate the economy? I said, No. I am not an economist, but every economist I have read on this tax package says that is one of the least stimulative— am I correct, Senator—one of the least stimulative provisions of the bill.

I want to know next week, when we are debating this, I would like at least one Republican—just one—it could be the minority leader *Mitch McConnell*, it could be the budget chairman *Judd Gregg*, it could be just one Republican—to give a passionate argument for why they insisted this be in the package. I would like to listen to it. I would like to hear it with my own ears. What was it about it that they thought was so important that they had to have it in the package? Because I know, as angry as I am with the President right now about some matters, I know the President did not insist this be in the package. I know enough about him to know that he didn't call everybody in the room and say, Oh, we forgot something. Let's make sure this tax extension includes people making over $1 million. I know he didn't give that speech. I want to know who did. Who did give it, because your constituents should know about it. And the American people have a right to know. That is one thing about our democracy, it is open. It could be more open. We could be like Britain where they all stand up and talk at one another in one of the rooms. It is very interesting. I find it very interesting to watch sometimes. We don't do that, but at least if the people of Britain want to know what their people are saying, they can hear them.

Somebody said this. I would like to know who, and where, and when. Was it in the Oval Office? Was it in the cloakroom? Because I am going to be forced to vote—because now, I think the Senator understands, we aren't going to have any amendments, so I am going to be forced to vote and have to choose, which is going to be a very tough choice, between extending tax cuts for 84 percent of the people in my state who make less than $75,000—which of course I want to do. Even though we have to borrow the money to do it, we can't not do it. The economic circumstances are such that we have to do it. But now, in order to get them help, I have to say yes to something that I have talked about—and I want to be serious about this; I am very serious about it—that, for me, borders on moral recklessness.

I have been criticized on both sides of this debate. How can you use words like this? I don't know. I went to Catholic school. We went to mass almost every week. Every week the priest would say, Don't take more than you need. Don't be greedy. Share with others. Did I go to the wrong school? So I would like to know. Maybe those lessons were missed on the other side. I don't normally speak like this. I have been criticized for it. I am very, very torn, because I like to be part of a team.

I understand, I say to the Senator from Vermont, that we can't have every package exactly the way we believe. I understand that. I have had to vote for some things that were hard for me to stomach, and I have done it because there were other good things in the bill. That is the way the process works. But I actually cannot remember a time on either an appropriations bill of this magnitude or a tax bill of this magnitude that we have been asked to cast a vote for something that on its face is so reckless, so unnecessary, so sort of in your face to the poor, in your face to the middle class. We are going to take our money. Don't you say a word about it.

Who said that? Did Warren Buffett come down here and ask for it? Did Boone Pickens come down here and ask for it? Did the Gateses come down here and ask for it? Who asked for it? Why do you think you deserve it, and what Senator put their name on it?

I have a few more things to say. I don't want to keep the Senator from Vermont tied up.

Mr. SANDERS. Quite the contrary. The Senator from Louisiana is making some very important points. I appreciate it and I look forward to hearing what she has to say.

Ms. LANDRIEU. Thank you. I wish to say a few other things about this whole situation, because the Senator from Vermont and I agree on some things and parts of this—obviously this part—but we had a big difference. I wanted to show this from my perspective.

I voted for the original tax cuts. I am not sure the Senator from Vermont did. There were very good reasons on both sides. I wish to take a minute, because I have, as I said, critics on both sides, and I want to explain—not explain, but share some thoughts about that and make something very clear.

I was one of 12 Democrats—there are only 7 of us left—in the Chamber today who voted for the Bush tax cuts. We were for the middle class and the poor and the wealthy. Everybody got income tax relief, capital gains tax relief, dividend tax relief. Senator *Lincoln* and I and others worked very hard to make sure that in that package—even though I would have designed it differently if I could have done it myself, but there are no czars around here. This is a democracy. I understand that. I have been doing it for 30 years. We worked hard to shape that package the best we could to direct it and target it to the middle class. There are many critics of that who say you didn't do it well enough. You didn't send it to the middle class. You sent it to the wealthy. I disagree. I think we did as well as we could to send it to the middle class, although the higher brackets were lowered as well. But I will tell my colleagues the big difference was, it was paid for when we voted for it. There was a $128 billion annual surplus. In other words, we were spending $128 billion less than we were taking in. What a happy time that was. We were paying for our Pell grants. We were paying for education. We were paying for health care. We had surpluses in Social Security, the Senator will remember, and we had a $128 billion surplus that year alone, and surpluses as far as the eye can see. This is before 9/11.

So the 12 of us—let me speak just for myself—I thought, what a situation this is. Democrats had taken the tough vote.

Not one Republican had voted for this budget reconciliation. As the Chair knows, as he was then in the House and took a tough vote with the Democrats to put us on that path, the middle class was expanding. Jobs were being created. We were creating millionaires. Yes, I love creating more millionaires. It is why I got into politics—one of the reasons. I like when people are successful. I love to hear stories about my constituents who came from poor families, whose mothers were household servants, whose fathers never went to high school—I love to hear about smart little girls from Gert Town who got straight A's in school, went down the street to Xavier University, got their premed degree, and then went on to become a doctor, and now they are millionaires. I don't decry that. I celebrate it. I have fought for them to get their scholarships—not individually but generally. It is what I do. It is what Senators and House Members do.

I am so mad at people saying to me, as a Democrat, that we don't like people who are rich; that we have something against them. Nothing could be further from the truth.

I love the book, *The Millionaire Next Door*. It talks about how it is a myth that most millionaires in America have inherited their money. The fact is, we have created such a great country over 250 years. We have actually found the way for poor people to go from nothing to huge wealth and to create a life-changing opportunity for their children and grandchildren. We celebrate it, write movies about it, and our libraries are full of books about it. There is nothing wrong with that.

So when we had a surplus, I thought we should give tax breaks and use some of that money. But, today, we are being asked to provide tax cuts, when the deficit is—I want to get this number correct because it is shocking—10 times greater than the surplus; it is $1.294 trillion. That is what the annual deficit is this year. When we did the tax cuts, we were generating a $128 billion surplus every year—surpluses as far as the eye could see. We thought maybe we should give a third of this bounty in tax cuts, and we made investments in other things. But, today, after what the Senator from Vermont has described as the economic inequality in the country, when we have no surplus in sight, the biggest, largest, most ferocious recession since the Great Depression, and we are running an annual deficit of $1.29 trillion—someone had the nerve on the other side of the aisle to say: Wait, before you close the deal, before you shut the door, before you stop the printing press, please put in the people in America who make over $1 million.

Now, for that $50 billion, there are lots of ways that we could save if we could correct this deal. I don't think we can. But if we could, as the Senator knows, do we have men and women in the military—does he know what their COLA will be this year? I think it is only 1.4 percent.

Mr. SANDERS. That is what my understanding is. I think a lot of the folks in the military are very upset about that.

Ms. LANDRIEU. Every person in uniform is only getting a COLA this year of 1.4 percent. Did anybody over there not think about this when they raised their hand to say let's give it to millionaires? Those in the military most certainly deserve a bonus. They are coming back without eyes or legs; they are leaving some of their limbs in Iraq and Afghanistan. Did anybody over there think about that?

The senior citizens for whom the Senator has been such an advocate are not seeing the kind of COLA they normally get. Talk about stimulus, I think every dollar you give to a senior citizen—wouldn't the Senator say—gets spent right away. They have to buy food with it. They are not going out perusing a yacht or an airplane they could or could not buy. They need to eat. They go to the corner drugstore; they need to get their medicine. They spend it. Yes, we give money to the poor on the Democratic side and the middle class because it is the right thing to do. It actually happens to be also the smart thing to do for the economy and for jobs.

So when people say the Senator has flip-flopped on taxes, I don't understand how to say it differently. I voted for tax cuts when we had a surplus. I am challenged about how to address this package—I most certainly want to extend it for the middle class and to extend help for the unemployed. People are unemployed not because they are lazy, for Heaven's sake. They are unemployed because there are no jobs for them. It is some of the longest term unemployment we have had in our Nation's history.

So the other side is making us feel—they say: We gave you the unemployment, so surely you should give us the tax breaks for millionaires. Is that really an equal trade? If somebody believes that actually—I have heard commentators say it on different networks. I have been on these news programs, and they say: You got the unemployment, so that is a fair trade.

If there is a Senator who thinks that, I would love them to say that next week. I think that would be great to have on the record. So this situation is what the Louisiana families in my state are facing. Obviously, I would like to provide tax relief for these families. We have less than 1.8 percent who are making over $200,000. I am checking right now to find out how many families in Louisiana actually make over $1 million. I was told it was 3,200. That number might be too high. The Senator from West Virginia told me that in his state it is 599 people who make over $1 million a year. Yet it looks like that is the package.

We are going to be in a tough situation, without amendments, having to vote for it. I will see what my constituents are saying over the weekend. I want to say one more thing about this inequity and turn it back over to the Senator from Vermont. Besides the other things that were put into the *Record* about the inequality, the challenges before our country right now, I came across some data, and I would like the Senator to be on the floor to listen to this.

Mr. SANDERS. I am not going anywhere. You can take as much time as you want.

Ms. LANDRIEU. I wasn't sure what his time was. I am chair of the Small Business Committee. I have many hearings, but I had one in the last three months and some of the testimony was startling to me. I wanted to share this with the Senator.

It is in the 2000 census data. Someone was testifying about why this recession was taking so long to get over. They were giving figures about the status of the economy and the wealth or incomes of broad sections of the population.

They said sort of off the cuff—like, ho-hum, today is Monday.

They said: By the way, the average net worth, the median net worth of households in America, the average—median net worth—not income but net worth—of households is $67,000. That is very interesting. I thought it would be higher than that. That is taking what you own minus everything you owe, and the difference is your net worth. I thought people might have more than that in terms of equity in their homes, a couple hundred thousand. That was concerning to me.

I said: Do you have that broken down by race, by any chance?

They said: Yes, ma'am.

I said: Would you share it? And they did. I will share it with you because I have not recovered from what I heard.

The gentlemen said to me: Well, for White families in America, the average median—50 percent more, 50 percent less—is $87,000. For Hispanic families, it is $8,000. For African-American families, it is $5,000.

I want to repeat that. Fifty percent of all families in America who are Caucasian, their net worth is $87,000 or less. For

Hispanic families in America, 50 percent of all Hispanic households, their net worth is $8,000. For African-American families today, in 2010—40 years after the peak of the civil rights movement and 150 years or so after the Civil War and all the things we think we have done to try to get people in a more equal position in our society—it is $5,000. That is including home equity—or home ownership, I mean. Without home ownership, that net worth for African-American families falls to $1,000.

So when people say people are in pain and suffering and anxious and they can't buy anything, you wonder why. There is no cushion in a recession like this. How brutal is a recession to people who have so little a cushion? For a middle-class family of any race, if you lose your job, you can get unemployment, you have some equity in your home, or maybe you have some savings you can fall back on. There is a cushion, and you can bounce back up. How brutal is this recession to millions of families in America who have no cushion? They are just hitting hard rock. They are hitting steel. There is no cushion there. You wonder why people are angry. You wonder why this Tea Party Movement is festering, why people are so angry. I understand that anger. I am so angry myself, I don't know what to do.

Mr. SANDERS. If I can interrupt my good friend, she is right. It is no great secret that her politics and mine aren't the same on many issues. She is down here speaking from her heart, coming from the State of Louisiana, which is not radically different from Vermont. We have a lot of struggling families.

I want to reiterate a point. She has been talking so effectively about the stress on the middle class and working families in her state and around the country. I want to reiterate this point. I am not here to pick on George W. Bush, but during his eight years, the wealthiest 400 Americans—pretty high up guys; that "ain't" the middle class no matter how broadly you define that—their income more than doubled—got that—while their income tax rate dropped almost in half from 1995 to 2007.

The wealthiest 400 Americans now earn an average of $345 million a year and pay an effective tax rate of 16.6 percent, on average. That is the lowest tax rate for wealthy individuals on record.

So the point is, Senator *Landrieu* and I are talking about the people out in the real world who are working longer hours for lower wages. Median family income has declined. People are scared that for the first time in our modern history their kids will have a lower standard of living than they had.

Is the Senator hearing that in Louisiana?

Ms. LANDRIEU. I am.

Mr. SANDERS. Senator *Landrieu* is asking a simple question, and millions of people are asking the same question. The wealthiest people are becoming much richer, the middle class is declining, and poverty is increasing. Who decided? Who said billionaires need an extended tax break and a reduction in the estate tax? It is a very simple question she is asking. It is a very profound question because it speaks to what this country is all about. I didn't mean to interrupt.

Ms. LANDRIEU. I thank the Senator from Vermont. I commend to my colleagues this report entitled "Income Inequality and the Great Recession" from Senator *Schumer* and the Joint Economic Committee. I ask unanimous consent that the Executive Summary be printed in the *Record*.

There being no objection, the material was ordered to be printed in the **RECORD**, as follows:

Income Inequality and the Great Recession
EXECUTIVE SUMMARY

This week, the U.S. Census Bureau will release new statistics on income inequality in the United States, allowing for an assessment of the impact of the Great Recession on our nation's income distribution. In preparation for that data release, the Joint Economic Committee (JEC) analyzed income inequality in the United States in the years preceding the Great Recession, and found:

Income inequality has skyrocketed. Economists concur that income inequality has risen dramatically over the past three decades.

Middle-class incomes stagnated under President Bush. During the recovery of the 1990s under President Clinton, middle-class incomes grew at a healthy pace. However, during the jobless recovery of the 2000s under President Bush, that trend reversed course. Middle-class incomes continued to fall well into the recovery, and never regained their 2001 high. The first year of the Great Recession dealt a sharp blow to middle-class families, who had not yet recovered from the pain of the last recession.

High levels of income inequality may precipitate economic crises. Peaks in income inequality preceded both the Great Depression and the Great Recession, suggesting that high levels of income inequality may destabilize the economy as a whole.

Income inequality may be part of the root cause of the Great Recession. Stagnant incomes for all but the wealthiest Americans meant an increased demand for credit, fueling the growth of an unsustainable credit bubble. Bank deregulation allowed financial institutions to create new exotic products in which the ever-richer rich could invest. The result was a bubble-based economy that came crashing down in late 2007.

Policymakers have a great deal of leverage in mitigating income inequality in order to stabilize the macro-economy. In the decades following the Great Depression, policy decisions helped keep income inequality low while allowing for continued economic growth. In contrast, policy decisions made during the economic expansion during the Bush administration failed to keep income inequality in check, and may have exacerbated the problem. Policymakers working to rebuild the economy in the wake of the Great Recession

should heed these lessons and pay particular attention to
policy options that mitigate economic inequality.

Ms. LANDRIEU. Mr. President, I want to go back to a
point about this so that I am not misunderstood. I guess no
matter what I say critics will take it and do what they will
with it, but I am not against tax cuts. I voted for them many
times in my life when we had surpluses. I have even been
pressured to vote for things, and have done so, when we
didn't have the surpluses, but they were targeted and focused
and there actually had been some rational thought attached
to where we might need to borrow some money and spend
it, such as in the stimulus package, because in that instance,
if we didn't get some spending going, we could slip further
into a recession. Even conservative economists counseled us
on parts of the stimulus package.

By the way, contrary to popular myth, that was about the
same size as this package. This package is actually larger. This
package is going to be $900 billion. The stimulus was $800-
something. It was less. But in that stimulus package about
a third was tax cuts. Remember that, Mr. President? A third
of that was tax cuts. It wasn't all just spending. But every
economist—conservative, liberal—said the government has
got to step up and spend in this economy because this place is
shutting down—meaning the country—and so we did.

People will still argue on the other side that was the
wrong thing to do and we shouldn't have done it. But I am
here to say that without the $2.8 billion in tax cuts and spend-

ing that went to Louisiana through that stimulus package—and my state legislature is struggling to balance the budget, as I speak; they have been in the budget committee over the past couple of weeks—I don't know where we would be today. I don't know how much went to Vermont or California or how much went to Colorado, but people say it was a failure. Well, let me say that $2.8 billion went to our state and it warded off some Draconian cuts that our cities and counties and parishes would have had to make, and it warded off tax increases so that Governors didn't have to raise taxes and mayors didn't have to raise taxes all over this country. Some of them have done that, but they have tried to limit it because they know how fragile this middle class is.

I am not unmindful of the importance of providing tax cuts when we can. But when we are asked to vote on a package that has a provision such as this, that borders on moral recklessness, I have to catch my breath and ask: Whose idea was this? I wish to know.

It is going to be a long weekend. It will be a long 30 hours of debate. I am glad the Senator from Vermont is going to make sure we take every one of those 30 hours postcloture, if we even get to cloture on this bill, because I think the American people are going to be waiting around to find out whose idea was that.

Mr. SANDERS. If I can interrupt the Senator from Louisiana, because she makes a very important point, we are a democracy and it is the American people who make the decisions. I know she shares with me the belief that the American people have to become engaged in this very important debate, which has a lot to do with the future of this country.

Senator *Landrieu* asks a very simple question, which I would like—and I think the American people would like—an answer to: Whose brilliant idea was it—at a time when we have seen an explosion in income and wealth to the people on top, while their tax rates have already gone down—that we drive up the national debt and ask our kids to pay higher taxes to pay off that debt in order to give tax breaks to people who don't need them? That is the question Senator *Landrieu* is asking. I think the American people need an answer to that, and my hope is that millions of Americans will start calling their Senators to ask that question.

Ms. LANDRIEU. Was it your idea? Whose idea was it?

Mr. SANDERS. Whose idea was it?

The irony here—and I think Senator *Landrieu* made this point as well—is that there are plenty of millionaires out there who say: I don't need it. I am more worried about the crumbling infrastructure or our kids out there than giving me a tax break I don't need. Thanks very much. That is what Warren Buffett has said. It is what Bill Gates has said. Ben Cohen of Ben & Jerry's has said it. Many millionaires have said it. We are giving some of these guys something they do not even want.

I want to thank Senator *Landrieu* very much, not only for her being here today—and please continue—but for raising these important issues.

Ms. LANDRIEU. One more point, and then I will turn this back over to the Senator.

I was on the Greta Van Susteren show last night. I have said Greta is always a tough interviewer, but she is fair, so I am happy to go on her program. And it was a tough interview. But we debated these things, and I think that is important. I think it is important to debate them here, on TV, and in town hall meetings. That is what democracy is all about. But she said to me: Senator, we are so frustrated. Nobody ever hears anybody say they want to cut spending, or they want to eliminate waste, fraud, and abuse. So let me concede this point. For me, I don't think we do talk enough about eliminating the waste, eliminating the fraud, and eliminating the abuse. I think we should spend more time, and I am going to commit myself to that, because I know the American people say: Every time we ask for a tax cut, you say we can't afford it. Why don't you cut some spending, et cetera.

Let me state that I voted for tax cuts. I am for tax cuts. I have even given tax cuts to people who do make more than the $75,000 or $100,000 or $250,000, when we had a surplus, when I thought it was the fiscally responsible thing to do. Other people can disagree, but this is the first time I am being asked to provide a tax cut for people earning over $1 million with this kind of deficit.

But I will say this: I am going to commit myself to trying to find places we can cut. I support the Federal freeze. I support it in appropriations this year. Senator *Inouye* is taking down on the appropriations level $8 billion below the President's budget, and if we need to go even further, perhaps we can. But we have to be careful where we cut, and I ask people to be rational about this. Do you want to cut Pell grants? I looked at this the other day, I say to the Senator from Vermont, particularly, because of Claiborne Pell. When the Pell grant went into effect, it was a grant to help kids go to school. That is still what it does. But in the 1970s, the Pell grant paid 100 percent of the average two-year college. It only pays 50 percent of that today. I think I remember it paid almost 60 percent of a four-year public college. It only pays like 40 percent or less than that today because we have not kept up with it.

A program such as the Pell grant is a powerful tool to lift the middle class, or lift the poor out of poverty and expand the middle class. So when we cut programs, let's be careful to cut the waste, to cut the abuse, but let's not cut the heart out of what we are arguing for—effective tools to expand the middle class—or we will never get out of this recession. Because I promise you, the few thousand people in this country—or few tens of thousands, I don't know how many who make more than $1 million a year—are not going to lift this country out of a recession. It is going to be the middle class. And if we don't help them get ahead, if we don't help them get training, this recession will go on for a long time.

Mr. SANDERS. I want to add the idea that when we think about cutting back on education—whether it is childcare, primary school, or college—we are simply cutting off our noses to spite our faces. The Senator is aware that where, at one time in this country, we used to lead the world in the number of our people who graduated college, we are now falling very significantly. How do you become a great economy if you don't have the scientists, the engineers, the teachers, the professionals out there, and many other countries around the world are having a higher percentage of their high school graduates going to college? That is something we have to address. Anyone who comes forward and says cut education is moving us in exactly the wrong direction.

Ms. LANDRIEU. Exactly. And I am for more accountability. If some of my colleagues on the other side think some of that money is being wasted or we are not getting our bang for the buck, don't come with an across-the-board cut to Pell grants, come with a plan to change it, saying these are the requirements for our universities: You have to graduate 65 percent of the kids who start or you have to have certain benchmarks before you can apply for these loans or for these grants.

This country is at a crossroads, and I know the President and his advisers understand the extraordinary challenges before this country. I hope the Members understand the economic danger, the minefield we are in here. We can't make too many mistakes here. There is no cushion left. There is no surplus left. We are down to below bottom. So when we do big things such as this—and this is a big thing, this $980 billion big package, it is almost $1 trillion—we need to do it the best way we can do it. We can't do it recklessly or frivolously. We can't do it for ideology, for gosh almighty's sakes.

I wish we could have fought harder for a better package. I have not yet decided how I am going to vote, but I have said if I vote, I am not voting quietly. I may vote yes, I may vote no, but I will vote with a loud voice about what I am concerned about, what I believe my constituents are concerned about, and I will try my best to help them, to support them, and to make the best decisions we can next week. But this has been troubling me, and so I wanted to come to the floor and speak about it, and I thank the Senator from Vermont.

I yield the floor.

Mr. SANDERS. I thank Senator *Landrieu* very much for coming, and I think she knows that on many issues her views and mine are different, but on this issue, I believe we are speaking for the overwhelming majority of the people, not just of Louisiana and Vermont but all over this country, who cannot understand why we give tax breaks to billionaires to drive up the deficit and the national debt at a time when the deficit and the debt are so large. I want to thank Senator *Landrieu* very much for her very articulate and heartfelt statements. I appreciate that very much.

Mr. President, I was mentioning a moment ago the great contrast about what is happening in our economy between the people on top and everybody else. I indicated that the top 400 families during the Bush Presidency alone saw their income more than double, while from 1995 to 2007, as their income tax rates dropped almost in half. So that is what is going on for the people on top, who would make out extremely well under this agreement between the President and the Republican leadership.

But I also talked about what is going on with the middle class and working families of this country. If you can believe it—and this is quite amazing—since December of 1999—and this was in a *Washington Post* article in January—there has been zero net job creation—zero net job creation. Middle-income households made less in 2008, when adjusted for inflation, than they did in 1999, and that number is sure to have declined further in 2009.

What does that mean? It means that when you look at a 10-year period—and people work very hard—in many instances—actually, in the vast majority of instances—you will have both husbands and wives working and still not making enough money to pay the bills. In fact, they have less money than they used to have.

When I was a kid growing up, the experience was that in the middle class one person—I know young people will not believe this, but it is true—years ago in the United States, before the great global economy, before robotics, before computers, one person could work 40 hours a week and earn enough money to pay the bills for the family. One person. Today, in Vermont and throughout this country, overwhelmingly you have husbands and wives both working. And in some instances they are working very long hours. But here is the rub: Today, a two-income family has less disposable income than a one-income family did 30 years ago because wages have not kept up with inflation, and because health care costs have soared, the cost of education has soared, housing has soared, and basic necessities have soared. This is a description of a country moving in the wrong direction.

Thirty years ago, a one-income family had more disposable income than a two-income family does today. And there are a lot of reasons for that. Maybe we will touch on them a little bit later. But one of them, in my view, has to do with our disastrous unfettered free trade policy, which has resulted in the shutdown of tens of thousands of factories in this country. Since 2001, we lost some 42,000 factories. We went from 17 million manufacturing jobs to less than 12 million manufacturing jobs, and in many instances, those were good jobs.

Where did they go?

Some shut down for a variety of reasons. But others shut down because we have trade laws that say you have to be a moron not to shut down in America because if you go to China, go to Vietnam, go to Mexico, go to a developing country, you pay workers there a fraction of what you are paying the workers in America. Why wouldn't you go? Then you bring your products right back into this country.

A couple of weeks ago, my wife and I did some Christmas shopping. Frankly—we went to a couple of stores—it is very hard to find a product manufactured in the United States of America. You do not have to have a Ph.D. in economics to understand we are not going to have a strong economy unless we have a strong manufacturing capability, unless companies are reinvesting in Colorado or Vermont, creating good jobs here. You do not have an economic future when virtually everything you are buying is coming from China or another country.

We are not just talking about low-end products. These are not sneakers or a pair of pants. This is increasingly high-tech stuff. We are forfeiting our future as a great economic nation unless we rebuild our industrial base and unless we create millions and millions of jobs producing the goods and the products we consume. We cannot continue to just purchase products from the rest of the world.

When we talk about the collapse of the middle class, it is important to also recognize the fact, as reported in *USA Today* September 17, 2009, "the incomes of the young and middle-aged—especially men—have fallen off a cliff since 2000, leaving many age groups poorer than they were even in the 1970s." The point being, for young workers, for example, when we had a manufacturing base in America in the 1940s, 1950s, 1960s, you could graduate high school and go out and get a job in a factory. Was it a glamorous job? No. Was it a hard job? Yes. Was it a dirty job? In some cases.

But if you worked in manufacturing, and especially if you had a union behind you, the likelihood is you earned wages to take your family into the middle class, you had decent health care coverage, and you might even have a strong pension. Where are all those jobs now? During the Bush years alone, we went from 17 million jobs in manufacturing to about 12 million jobs, a horrendous loss of manufacturing jobs. If you are a kid today in Colorado or Vermont and you are not of a mind, for whatever reason, to go to college—30 or 40 years ago you could go out, get a job in factory, and make some money. Today, what are your options? You can get a minimum wage job at McDonald's or maybe at Walmart, where benefits are minimal or nonexistent. That is a significant transition of the American economy.

I wish to tell you something else, when we talk about manufacturing. It did not get a whole lot of publicity, but it is worth reporting. The good news is, we have recently seen—after the loss of many thousands of jobs in the automobile industry—we have seen the auto companies, Chrysler and others, starting to rehire. What I think has not been widely reported is, the wages of the new workers who are being hired are 50 percent of the wages of the older workers in the plant. You are going to have workers working side by side, where an older worker who has been there for years is making $28 an hour, and right next to him a new hire is making $14 an hour. If you understand that the automobile industry was perhaps the gold standard for manufacturing in America, what do you think is going to happen to the wages of blue-collar workers in the future?

If all you can get with a union behind you in automobile manufacturing is $14 an hour today, what are you going to make in Colorado or in Vermont? Are you going to make $10 an hour or $11 an hour? Is that enough money on which to raise a family? Are you going to have any benefits? Unlikely.

That is what happens when your manufacturing base disappears and that, to a significant degree, in my view, is a result of a disastrous trade policy. I have to tell you—and I think in hindsight most people agree I was right—when I was in the House and all the corporations in the world were telling us how great NAFTA would be, free trade with Mexico, I did not buy it. I was right. They would say: Oh, it is going to be even better. We will have free trade with China. Think about how large China is and all the American products they are going to buy over there to create all kinds of jobs in the United States. I never believed it for a moment.

I will tell you a story. I was in China a number of years ago and as part of a congressional delegation we went to visit Walmart in China. The Walmart store, amazingly enough, looked a lot like Walmart in America—different products, but it looked like the same style. You walk up and down the aisles and you see all these American products. I remember Wilson basketballs, Procter & Gamble soap products—different products there for the Chinese, but a lot of the products were American products. They looked pretty familiar.

I asked the guy who was there with us who was, I believe, the head of Walmart Asia—the guy in charge of all the Walmarts in Asia—I asked him a simple question: Tell me, how many of these American company products are actually manufactured in the United States?

He was a little bit sheepish and a little bit hesitant and he said: Well, about 1 percent. Obviously, what everybody knew, it is a lot cheaper for the American companies to set up plants in China, hire Chinese workers at 50 cents an hour, 75 cents an hour, whatever it is, and have them build the product for the Chinese markets than it is to pay American workers $15 an hour, $20 an hour, provide health insurance, deal with the union, deal with the environment. That is not a great revelation. I think anybody could have figured that one out. But the big money interests around here pushed it and Congress and President Clinton, at that time, signed it and we were off and running.

When we look at why the middle class is in the shape it is—and it is important to make sure everybody understands it because one of the things that happens in this world, it is human nature I suppose, is that people feel very guilty and responsible if they are not taking care of their families. Right now we know, with unemployment so high—this is not just cold statistics we are throwing out. These are people who not only were earning an income that supported their families, they had a sense of worth. Every human being wants to be productive. They want to produce something. They want to be part of something. They want to go to work, earn a paycheck, bring it home. You feel good about that.

Do you know what it does to somebody's sense of human worth when suddenly you are sitting home watching the TV all day, you can't go out and earn a living? It destroys people. People become alcoholic. People commit suicide. People have mental breakdowns because they are not utilizing their skills. They are no longer being a productive member of society. That is what unemployment is about.

I think one of the reasons unemployment is so high, one of the reasons the middle class is collapsing, has a lot to do with these disastrous trade policies. I have to tell you, as we have been talking about all day long, these policies, these tax breaks, all this stuff emanates from corporate leaders whose sense of responsibility is such that they want themselves to become richer, they want more and more profits for their company, but they could care less about the needs of the American people.

I remember there was one CEO of a large, one of our largest American corporations, and he said: When I look at the future of General Electric, I see China, China, China, and China. By the way, we ended up bailing out that particular corporation. He didn't look to China to get bailed out, he looked to the taxpayers of this country.

But the word has to get out to corporate America, they are going to have to start reinvesting in the United States of America. They are going to have to start building the products and the goods the American people need rather than run all over in search of cheap labor. That is an absolute imperative if we are going to turn this economy around.

According to a *Boston Globe* article published on January 19, 2010—let me quote what they say. Again, I am trying to document here what is happening to the working class of America because I do not want individual workers, somebody who may be hearing this on the TV, the radio, to say: It is my fault. There is something wrong with me because I can't go out and get a job.

You are not alone. The entire middle class is collapsing. Our economy is shedding millions and millions of jobs. I know there are people out there trying hard to find work, but that work is just not there. That is why we have to rebuild the economy and create jobs. This is what the *Boston Globe* said last year: "The recession has been more like a depression for blue-collar workers. . . . "

This is an important point to be made here. When we talk about the economy we kind of lump everybody together. That is wrong. The truth is right now in the economy people on top are doing very well. The unemployment rate for upper income people is very low. They are doing OK. That as opposed, as this *Boston Globe* article points out, to what is happening to blue-collar workers: "The recession has been more like a depression for blue-collar workers, who are losing jobs much more quickly than the nation as a whole. . . . "

This is the working class of America. " . . . the Nation's blue-collar industries have slashed one in six jobs since 2007. . . . " Let me repeat that. It is just astronomical, a fact.

". . . the nation's blue-collar industries [manufacturing] have slashed 1 in 6 jobs since 2007, compared with about 1 in 20 for all industries, leaving scores of the unemployed competing for the rare job opening in construction or manufacturing, with many unlikely to work in those fields again."

Never.

"Up to 70 percent of unemployed blue-collar workers have lost jobs permanently, meaning their old jobs won't be there when the economy recovers."

That is the *Boston Globe*, January 19, 2010. When we talk about the economy, what we have to do is understand that blue-collar workers, middle-class, young workers are hurting very much. In the context, again, of the debate we are now having, the discussion of whether we should approve the agreement reached between the President and the Republicans on taxes, the idea of not significantly investing in our economy but, rather, giving tens of billions of dollars to the very rich in more tax breaks makes no sense to many of us.

When we talk about why people are angry, why people, when asked the question by pollsters: Do you think America is moving in the right direction, and overwhelmingly they think not, let me tell you why they think not. This is just during the Presidency of President Bush from 2001 through 2008. During that period alone—and by the way, the pain is certainly continuing right now. I do not mean to suggest otherwise. During those eight years of Bush, over 8 million Americans slipped out of the middle class and into poverty.

Today, nearly 40 million Americans are living in poverty; 7.8 million Americans lost their health insurance, and that is continuing.

A recent study came out and suggests that the uninsured now are about 50 million Americans. Fifty million Americans have no health insurance now. We hope health insurance reform will make a dent on that. I think it will. But as of today, without the major provisions of health care reform being implemented, 50 million Americans are without any health insurance.

During that period—and we have not talked about this a whole lot—there is another thing going on in the economy for the working class. Years and years ago, if you worked in a manufacturing plant, you had a union, you stood a reasonable chance of having a pension—a pension. During the Bush years, 3.2 million workers lost their pensions, and about half of American workers in the private sector have no pension coverage whatsoever. The idea today of having a defined benefit pension plan significantly paid for by your employer is going the way of the dinosaur. That is just not there anymore.

Workers are more and more dependent on Social Security, which has been there for 75 years, which we have to protect and demand that it will be there another 75 years because right now millions of workers are losing their pensions. I mean, I am throwing these statistics out, and the reason I am doing that is I want people to appreciate that if you are hurting now, stop being ashamed. It is not, yeah, we can all do better. Every one of us can do better. But you are in an economy which is contracting, especially for the middle class and working families.

According to an article in *USA Today*, from the year 2,000 to 2007, middle-class men—women have done better— middle-class men experienced an 11.2 percent drop in their incomes—a reduction of $7,700 after adjusting for inflation. Middle-class women in this age group saw a 4.8 percent decline in their incomes as well. So they did pretty badly, but the men did even worse. So what we are seeing is an understanding of why people are angry and why people think this country is moving in the wrong direction.

I think most people understand that today our country is experiencing the worst economic crisis since the Great Depression of the 1930s. It is important to say that because, again, it is hard enough when you do not have a job, when you do not have income, when your dignity and self-respect are declining, but I don't want people to be banging their own heads against the wall blaming themselves for all of the problems. Something has gone on in the Nation as a whole. You are not in this alone. When we talk about working-class families all across the country seeing a decline in their income, it is not because people are lazy, it is not because people do not work hard, it is not because people are not trying to find jobs. What we have is an economy which is rotting in the middle, and we have to change the economy.

If there is anything we can say about the American people, we work hard. We, in fact, work longer hours than do the people of any other country, industrialized country, on Earth.

We are not a lazy people. We are a hard-working people. If the jobs are there, people will take them. If people have to work 60 hours a week or 70 hours a week, that is what they will do. But we have to rebuild this economy. We do not need tax breaks for billionaires. We need to create jobs for the middle class of this country so that we can put people back to work.

Let me take a few minutes to discuss how we got to where we are today and, in my view, what policies we need to move this country forward to create the kinds of jobs we desperately need.

Let's take a quick look back to where we were in January of 2009—it seems like a long time ago but just a couple of years ago. That was the last month of the administration of President Bush. In that month, we lost over 700,000 jobs. That is an absolutely incredible number. In fact, during the last six months of the Bush Presidency, we lost over 3½ million jobs, all of which was caused by the greed and recklessness and illegal behavior on Wall Street.

Our gross domestic product, which is the total sum of all our economy produces, had gone down by nearly 7 percent during the fourth quarter of 2008. That was the biggest decline in more than a quarter century. Some $5 trillion of America's wealth evaporated in a 12-week period, as the people in Vermont and all over this country saw the value of their homes, retirement savings, and stocks plummet.

I want to say just one word again about Wall Street greed because I think for a variety of reasons we just do not talk about it enough. What you had was a situation in which a small number of folks at the head of huge financial institutions, through their greed, through the development of very reckless policies, through illegal behavior, through pushing out financial instruments which turned out in some cases to be worthless—as a result of all of that, they plunged this country into the worst recession we have seen since the Great Depression. That is at the end of the Bush Administration.

It is very important to understand that the Wall Street crisis took us over the wall in terms of precipitating the severe recession we are in, but we have to remember that during those previous eight years, as I mentioned earlier, the middle class was also shrinking. So it was not: Oh my goodness, everything is going great. Then you got the Wall Street disaster, and now we are in the midst of a terrible recession. This trend of a middle-class collapse went on long before Bush—precipitated significantly during the Bush years, but it went on before as well, not just during the Bush years.

Over the eight-year period of President Bush, from 2001 to 2009, we lost over 600,000 private sector jobs. We lost over 600,000 private sector jobs, and only 1 million net new jobs were created, all of them in the government sector. So for my friends, my Republican colleagues, to tell us that we need more tax breaks for the very rich because that is going to create jobs—that is what trickle-down economics is all about—I would say to them: You had your chance. It failed. In case you don't know, losing over 600,000 private sector jobs in eight years is not good. That is very, very bad. That is an economic policy that has failed. We don't need to look at that movie again. We saw it. It stunk. It was a bad movie. Bad economic policy. More tax breaks for the rich is not what our economy needs. In fact, what every economist will tell you is that is the least effective way to create jobs.

During the Bush era, median income dropped by nearly $2,200. That means that a family in the middle, over an eight-year period, saw their income drop by $2,200 during the eight years of Bush.

I say all of these things just to tell you that we are not where we are today just because of the Wall Street crisis. That took us over the cliff. That made a very bad situation much, much worse. But it has been going on for a long time. It has gone on before Bush. It has gone on after Bush.

During the eight years of Bush, over 8 million Americans slipped out of the middle class and into poverty. We don't talk about poverty in America anymore. We don't talk about the homelessness in America very much anymore. Trust me, it is there. It is three blocks away from where I am speaking right now, a very large homeless shelter. It is in small towns in Vermont where people tell me that for the first time they are seeing more and more families with kids needing emergency shelter because they can't afford housing. In Vermont, a lot of people have low-wage jobs making 10 bucks an hour, and it is hard to find a decent apartment or pay a mortgage on $10 an hour. That is true certainly all over this country. Homelessness is going up.

During the Bush years, nearly 8 million Americans lost their health insurance. One of the issues I will talk about in a little while is health care. It is related to everything. We are the only country in the industrialized world that does not guarantee health care to all people as a right of citizenship. According to Harvard University, 45,000 Americans will die this year because they lack health insurance and are not getting to a doctor when they should.

During the Bush administration, about 5 million manufacturing jobs disappeared, as companies shut down plants in the United States and moved to China, Mexico, Vietnam, and other low-wage countries. As I mentioned earlier, it is profoundly important to understand what is going on in America. In January 2000, we had over 17 million manufacturing jobs in this country. By January 2009, we had about 12 million. That is 17 million to about 12 million in eight years. That is the loss of some 5 million manufacturing jobs—a 29 percent reduction—and the fewest number of manufacturing jobs since the beginning of World War II.

Under President Bush, our trade deficit with China more than tripled and the overall trade deficit nearly doubled.

Again, the point I am making now in the context of this agreement is that we need agreements now that do not give tax breaks to millionaires or billionaires, that do not lower the estate tax, which is applicable only to the top three-tenths of 1 percent. We need an agreement that rebuilds our infrastructure, rebuilds our manufacturing base, and creates the millions of good-paying jobs the American people desperately want.

Again, I think the point has to be made—and I have to make it over and over—that when you look at the economy, it is one thing to say everybody is hurting. You know, sometimes that happens. A terrible hurricane comes through and knocks down everybody's home. Well, the hurricane that has hit America for the last 10, 20 years has not impacted everybody; it has impacted the working class, it has impacted the middle class. The people on top are doing better than they ever were. Our friends on Wall Street whose greed and illegal behavior caused this recession are now making more money than they ever did, after being bailed out by the middle class of this country.

During the Bush years, the wealthiest 400 Americans saw their incomes more than double. Do you really think that after seeing a doubling of their incomes under the Bush years, these people are in desperate need of another million-dollar-a-year tax break? In 2007, the 400 top income earners in this country made an average of $345 million in one year. That is a pretty piece of change. That is the average, $345 million. In terms of wealth, as opposed to income, the wealthiest 400 Americans saw an increase in their wealth of some $400 billion during the Bush years. Imagine that. During an eight-year period, the top 400 wealthiest people each saw an increase, on average, of about $1 billion apiece. Together, these 400 families have a collective net worth of $1.27 trillion. Does anybody in America really believe these guys need another tax break so that our kids and our grandchildren can pay more in taxes because the national debt has gone up? I do not think most Americans believe that. That is why, in my view, most Americans are not supporting this agreement.

Let me also say that when we look at what is going on around the rest of the world, what we have to appreciate is that in the United States today—again, this is not something we can be proud of; it is something we have to address—we have the most unequal distribution of wealth and income of any other country on Earth.

I remember talking not so long ago to somebody from Scandinavia. I think it was Finland. He was saying: Of course, we have rich people in our country, but there is a level at which they would become embarrassed.

America now has a situation where the CEOs of large corporations make over 260 times more than the average American worker. In many other countries, everybody wants to be rich, but there is a limit. You can't become a billionaire stepping over children sleeping on the street. That is not what this country is supposed to be about. Enough should be enough.

In 2007, the top 1 percent earned 23.5 percent of all income. In the 1970s, that number was about 8 percent. In the 1990s, it was approximately 16 percent. Now it is 23.5 percent. So the people on top are getting a bigger and bigger chunk of all income. Furthermore, it is not only the top 1 percent, there are economists who ask: You think the top 1 percent are doing well? It is really the top one-tenth of 1 percent. If you can believe this, the top one-tenth of 1 percent—and I don't know how many people that is, you can do the arithmetic, 300 million into one-tenth of 1 percent—took in 11 percent of total income in 2007. One-tenth of 1 percent earned 11 percent of all income in America in 2007.

In the 1970s, the top 1 percent only made something like 8 percent of total income. In the 1980s it rose to 10 to 14 percent. In the late 1990s, it was 15 percent to 19 percent. In 2005 it passed 21 percent. And in 2007, the top 1 percent received 23 percent of all the income earned in this country.

People should be mindful of this fact: The last time that type of income disparity took place was in 1928. I think we all know what happened in 1929. That is the point Senator *Landrieu* was making a while back. What she understands, quite correctly, is if working people, the vast majority of the people, don't have the income to spend money to buy products and goods and services, we can't create the jobs. If all of the money or a big chunk of the money ends up with a few people on top, there is a limit to how many limousines you can have and how many homes you can have and how many yachts you can have. So when we hit a situation where so few have so much, it is not only a moral issue, it is also an economic issue.

A strong and growing middle class goes out, spends money, and creates jobs. Grossly unequal distribution of income and wealth creates more economic shrinkage and loss of jobs because people just don't have the disposable income to go out and buy and create jobs.

To add insult to injury in terms of this agreement negotiated by the President and Republicans, while the very wealthiest people became much wealthier and the deficit soared—and under President Bush the national debt almost doubled—what else happened? The tax rates for the very rich went down. The rich got richer; tax rates went down. This was a result not only of the tax breaks for the rich initiated during the Bush administration but also, quite frankly, tax policy that took place before President Bush. The result is that from 1995 to 2007, from the latest statistics we have, the effective Federal tax rate—what people really pay—for the top 400 income earners was cut almost in half. So these cry babies, these multimillionaires and billionaires, these people who are making out like bandits, they are crying and crying and crying, but the effective tax rate for the top 400 income earners was cut almost in half from 1995 to 2007.

The point that needs to be made is, when is enough enough? That is the essence of what we are talking about. Greed, in my view, is like a sickness. It is like an addiction. We know people who are on heroin. They can't stop. They destroy their lives. They need more and more heroin. There are people who can't stop smoking. They have problems with nicotine. They get addicted to cigarettes. It costs them their health. People have problems with food. We all have our share of addictions. But I would hope that these people who are worth hundreds of millions of dollars will look around them and say: There is something more important in life than the richest people becoming richer when we have the highest rate of childhood poverty in the industrialized world. Maybe they will understand that they are Americans, part of a great nation which is in trouble today. Maybe they have to go back to the Bible, whatever they believe in, and understand there is virtue in sharing, in reaching out; that you can't get it all.

I think this is an issue we have to stay on and stay on and stay on. This greed, this reckless, uncontrollable greed is almost like a disease which is hurting this country terribly. How can anybody be proud to say they are a multimillionaire and are getting a huge tax break when one-quarter of the kids in this country are on food stamps? How can one be proud of that? I don't know.

It is not only income, it is wealth. The top 1 percent owns more wealth than the bottom 90 percent. During the Bush years, the wealthiest 400 Americans saw their wealth increase by some $400 billion. How much is enough?

All of these things are related to the agreement the President and Republicans worked out because we are all concerned about the national debt and deficit. In terms of the Federal budget, when President Bush first took office, he inherited a $236 billion surplus in 2001 and a projected 10-year surplus of $5.6 trillion. That is what Senator *Landrieu* was discussing. But then some things happened. We all know that 9/11 was not his fault, but what happened is, we went to war in Afghanistan. We went to war in Iraq. The war in Iraq was the fault of President Bush, something I certainly did not support, nor do I think most Americans supported. The war in Iraq, by the time our last veteran is taken care of, will probably end up costing us something like $3 trillion, adding enormously to our national debt.

So when we talk about Iraq, it is not only the terrible loss of life that our soldiers and the Iraqi people have experienced, let's not forget what it has done to the deficit and the national debt. We did not pay for the war in Iraq. We just put it on the credit card.

President Bush gave out $700 billion in tax cuts for the wealthiest 1 percent of Americans. Where was the offset? There was none. He gave them tax breaks. That is it. It adds to the national debt.

The President and Republicans supported a $400 billion Medicare Part D prescription drug program. I have always believed we need a strong prescription drug program for seniors. But the program that was passed was written by the pharmaceutical industry, written by the insurance companies, and is nowhere near as cost-effective as it could be. As the President undoubtedly knows, we are not even negotiating prescription drug prices with the drug companies, a great expense and great cost to the American people, where drug prices are now much more expensive under Medicare Part D than they are in terms of what the Veterans' Administration or the Department of Defense purchases. So we passed that, unpaid for. Great idea. Just another $400 billion prescription drug program unpaid for.

Then we bailed out Wall Street. The original cost was $700 billion. A lot of that has been paid back, but there is expense there as well.

So we add all these things together, and normal governmental growth, and it turns out that the Bush administration turned a $236-billion-a-year surplus into a $1.3-trillion-a-year deficit. More or less, that is where we are right now. In fact, the national debt nearly doubled under President Bush, going from $5.7 trillion to $10.6 trillion in 2009 and now we are at $13.8 trillion, borrowing huge sums of money from China and other countries in order to maintain our existence. That is where we are.

Have we been seeing in recent months some improvements in the economy? We sure have. There has been some job growth. Nowhere near enough. But we are surely not losing 700,000 jobs a month. We are seeing some growth. But we need to do much better.

That takes me back to an issue I feel strongly about and one on which I want to say a few words. In this agreement the President negotiated with Republicans, there is a substantial sum of money going into various types of business tax breaks. The theory, which has certainly some validity, is that these business tax breaks will create jobs. The problem is that right now, businesses, the large corporations at least, are already sitting on a huge bundle of money that they are not spending. The reason they are not investing that money is they perceive that working families don't have the money to buy their products and services.

In saying this, I am not alone. I think most economists agree there is a far more effective way we can create jobs rather than just a number of tax breaks going to businesses. I touched on this point before. I want to get into a little bit more detail.

For this I am indebted to a very fine book written by an old friend of mine, Arianna Huffington. The title of her book is *Third World America*. She used these words because basically the theme of her book is, if we do not get our act together in terms of infrastructure, in terms of education, in terms of health care, that is where we are headed. We are headed in the direction of being a Third World nation.

She has an interesting chapter which deals with one very important part of what is going on in America, and that is the crumbling of our infrastructure. She writes:

"From 1980 to 2005, the miles traveled by automobiles increased 94 percent—for trucks mileage increased 105 percent—yet there was only a 3.5 percent increase in highway lane miles."

More and more cars, more and more traveling. We are not building roads.

But you don't need these numbers to know that our roads are badly congested.

Anybody who lives around Washington knows our roads are congested. It takes hours to get to work sometimes.

You see it and experience it every day.

According to the American Society of Civil Engineers' infrastructure report card—and this is where we should be investing, not tax breaks for the rich—Americans spend 4.2 billion hours a year stuck in traffic. Think about that, 4.2 billion hours a year stuck in traffic, at a cost of $78 billion a year. Think about all of the pollution, all of the greenhouse gas emissions, all of the frustration, all of the anxiety, all of the road rage. People are stuck on roads because our transportation system is totally inadequate, our roads, our public transportation.

She then makes another interesting point. When we talk about automobile accidents, what do we usually think? We think somebody is driving recklessly, maybe they are drunk. Those are serious issues. But she writes: "In studying car crashes across the country, the Transportation Construction Coalition determined that badly maintained or managed roads are responsible for $217 billion a year in car crashes, far more than headline-grabbing, alcohol-related accidents or speed-related pileups."

In other words, if you want to know why we are seeing automobile crashes, the issue of bad roads is even more significant than drunk drivers or people who are reckless drivers. I can remember—I think everybody has the same story—I was driving on a road in Vermont, and, whoops, there was a huge pothole, and the car went into it. It cost a few hundred dollars to repair the car. So we as a nation are spending billions of dollars repairing our cars because our roads are not in good shape. When there is a traffic jam, people are emitting all kinds of greenhouse gas emissions. You are wasting gas. You are wasting money. If we invested in our transportation system, we could go a long way to addressing that.

When we talk about transportation—and, by the way, again, I bring this issue up because, in the bill agreed to by the President and the Republican leadership, to the best of my knowledge, not one penny—not one penny—is going into infrastructure, which, to me, does not make any sense at all.

Again, Arianna Huffington writes: "America's railway system is speeding down the tracks in reverse. It is one of the few technologies that has actually regressed over the past 80 years."

Regressed. I am not talking about China, where they are building all these high-speed rail lines. Our rail situation in terms of the amount of time it takes to go from location one to location two has actually gotten longer.

She writes:

"Tom Vanderbilt of Slate.com—"

Which is a very good Web site—

"came across some pre-World War II train timetables and made a startling discovery. Many train rides in the 1930s, 40s, and 50s took less time than those journeys would take today."

Can you imagine that? In the 1930s, 1940s, and 1950s, people were able to get on a train and get to their destination in less time than is the case today.

For instance, in 1934, the Burlington Zephyr would get you from Chicago to Denver—from Chicago to Denver—in around 13 hours. The same trip takes 18 hours today.

I do not know if the Presiding Officer is familiar with the Burlington Zephyr, which is a train that goes from Chicago to Denver, but what this writer is pointing out is that in 1934 it took 13 hours to make that trip. Do you know how long it takes today? It takes 18 hours. So we are moving in the wrong direction.

I know in Vermont—I do not have any statistics right in front of me but I can tell you—I believe very strongly—it takes longer to get from the southern part of the state to the northern part of the state than it used to, and the frequency of the trips is less than they used to be.

The trip from Chicago to Minneapolis via the Olympian Hiawatha, in the 1950s, took about 4½ hours. Today, via Amtrak's train, the journey takes more than 8 hours.

It used to be 4½. So in terms of our public transportation, not only are we neglecting, not only are we not moving forward, we are actually moving backwards.

At the moment, the only high-speed train in the United States is Amtrak's Acela, which travels the Washington, New York, Boston line.

And she writes: "And I use the term 'high-speed' very loosely. While in theory the trains have a peak speed of 150 miles per hour, the average speed on that train is just about 71 miles per hour."

Once again, I read some statistics before, pointing out that China is building thousands and thousands of miles of high-speed rail. And here in the United States we are moving backwards. It is taking us a longer time for various train rides than used to be the case.

But it is not just trains. It is not just our roads. It is not just our bridges.

Well, it is also our bridges. Let me say a word on bridges. I think we all remember four years ago, I think it was, the terrible tragedy in the Minneapolis area, when one of their major bridges collapsed and a number of people lost their lives. That got the front-page headlines all over this country. I know in Vermont we closed down bridges. They are not safe to travel.

According to the Department of Transportation, one in four of America's bridges is either structurally deficient or functionally obsolete. The numbers are even worse when it comes to bridges in urban areas, where one in three bridges is deficient—no small matter given the high levels of passengers and freight traffic in our Nation's cities.

So a huge amount of traffic—in urban areas one in three bridges is deficient, and in rural areas such as Vermont, one in four.

How are these bridges going to be rebuilt? It is likely not going to be done by local and state governments that right now are experiencing enormous economic crises. If it is going to be done, it is going to have to be done here at the Federal level.

I have to say that in Vermont we saw some significant improvements as a result of the stimulus package. In fact, in Vermont, recently, we have put more money in rebuilding our roads and bridges with very good success. I think the people of Vermont see the difference. In the last couple years, directly as a result of the stimulus package, we have made significant improvements on a number of bridges but nowhere near enough.

The point I want to make is that with our infrastructure collapsing, with the American Society of Civil Engineers suggesting we need to spend $2.2 trillion in the next five years just to maintain where we are, we have an agreement before us which puts zero dollars in infrastructure. According to this book:

We need to invest $850 billion over the next 50 years to get all of America's bridges into good shape.

Trust me, we are not coming anywhere near that right now.

But it is not just our roads. It is not just our public transportation. It is not just our bridges. When we talk about infrastructure, we also have to talk about dams.

On March 16, 2006, the Ka Loko Dam in Kilauea, Hawaii, collapsed, and seven people died when the Ka Loko Dam breached after weeks of heavy rain, sending 1.6 million tons of water downstream.

Dams are a vital part of America's infrastructure. They help provide for drinking water, irrigation, and agriculture, and generate much needed power, and often offer protection from floods. Yet our dams are growing old. There are more than 85,000 dams in America, and the average age is 51 years. At the same time, more and more people are moving into developments located below dams that require significantly greater safety standards. But we have had a hard time keeping up with the increase in the so-called high-hazard dams. Indeed, we are falling further and further behind.

So the point here is, we have a major agreement. People are concerned about creating jobs. We are investing zero in our infrastructure, and dams are a very important part of our infrastructure, as are levees. And I suspect Senator *Landrieu*, who was here a little while ago, would have something to say about levees.

All right. So we are talking about an infrastructure which is collapsing. We are talking about China investing far more in terms of their GDP into infrastructure improvement than we are. We are talking about being in the midst of a major recession, where we desperately want to grow jobs, and yet this proposal does not add one cent into our infrastructure.

Now, again, I am going back to the very good book written by Arianna Huffington called *Third World America*. She writes:

"As bad as America's sewers, roads, bridges, dams, and water power systems are, they pale in comparison to the crisis we are facing in our schools. I am not talking about the physical state of our dilapidated public school buildings, although the National Education Association estimates that it would take $322 billion to bring America's school buildings into good repair."

I have been in schools in Vermont and elsewhere which were old and crumbling, and I have been in schools which are new and state of the art. I think anyone who has seen the contrast in terms of the attitude of the students in those types of schools will understand it is important to give these kids good places in which to learn and to grow. It means a lot to them when they see a building that is new that has state-of-the-art equipment, as opposed to one that is crumbling. It suggests to them what we as a society feel about them.

Arianna Huffington writes: "Nothing is quickening our descent into Third World status faster than our resounding failure to properly educate our children. This failure has profound consequences for our future, both at home and as we look to compete with the rest of the world in the global economy."

She writes: "Historically, education has been the great equalizer."

That is certainly the case.

That has been the incredible virtue of our public school system.

What we have given kids (my father did not graduate from high school. My mother did. That was it.), given millions of young people, is the opportunity to get a good education in school and be able to go to college and use their potential. The springboard to the middle class and beyond has been education. It was a promise we made to all of our people.

What we as a nation said is, regardless of your income, we are going to provide you with the best possible education in order to succeed in life. That is something extraordinary, that no matter what your income is, we are going to provide you with a great education. As a kid, I went to public schools, and I did have a very good education.

But something has gone terribly wrong in recent years, and we have slipped further and further behind many other countries. Among 30 developed countries ranked by the Organisation for Economic Co-operation and Development—that is the OECD—the United States ranked 25th in math and 21st in science.

So 25th in math, 21st in science.

Even the top 10 percent of American students—our best and brightest—ranked only 24th in the world in math literacy.

There was another study, I think probably just a more updated OECD study, that came out just the other day, reported in the *New York Times*, where kids in Shanghai were leading the world in these types of tests as compared to our own students. They have better schools, better teachers, more investments in their education. And there is a culture there. There is a culture. It is not fair to blame the kids.

Does anyone seriously believe in the United States of America we take intellectual development seriously? I was reading today—I do not remember the guy's name, who it was—a basketball player or a baseball player just signing a contract for untold tens of millions of dollars. Yet you have teachers starting off at $30,000, $32,000. Is anyone going to suggest in a serious way we reward people who become childcare workers or teachers?

We have childcare workers taking care of little kids—which may be the most important job in our society because there is the brain development that takes place between zero and three that has a large part to do with what a human being becomes— people leaving early childhood education in order to move up the economic ladder and get a job at McDonald's because pay is so low, benefits are so low. What are we doing as a nation?

Huffington writes: "A National Assessment of Educational Progress report found that just 33 percent of U.S. fourth graders and 32 percent of eighth graders were proficient in reading."

Et cetera, et cetera, et cetera.

So I think her point is that if we are not going to become a Third World nation, we have to start investing in this country—in our physical infrastructure, in our human infra-structure, and in our educational infrastructure.

Let me give you some examples of what this means in real terms. Today, unemployment in our country—the offi-cial unemployment rate is 9.8 percent. For those without a high school diploma, it is 15.6 percent, compared to 5.6 per-cent for college graduates. Mr. President, 67 percent of high school graduates do not have enough of the skills required for success in college and the 21st century workforce.

As many as 170,000 high school graduates each year are prepared to go on to college but cannot afford that. Let me repeat that. About 170,000 young people in this country, who graduate high school, who want to go to college, are unable to do it because they cannot afford it.

Are we nuts? What are we doing in wasting the extraordinary intellectual potential of all of these young people?

What we are saying to them is because you don't have the money and because college is so expensive, and because our Federal Government is more busy giving tax breaks to billionaires and fighting two wars, we are not investing in you.

That makes no sense at all. When you invest in your kids, you are investing in the future of America. They are America. And if they are not well educated, how are they going to become productive members of society? How are we going to compete against China and Europe and other countries around the world that are investing in education?

Here is something we don't talk about enough: The fastest-growing occupations are those that require higher levels of education and greater technical competency. So we have a problem—it is true in Vermont and it is true all over the country—which is we have jobs out there, good jobs, and those jobs cannot be filled because our young people don't have the job skills to fill them. How absurd is that?

I remember there was a piece in one of the papers, I think it was in Ohio, where after the worst of the recession, a lot of layoffs—I think it was Ohio—they were beginning to hire workers and these were for sophisticated, high-tech jobs. They brought workers in and brought them in and brought them in, and they couldn't come up with the number of workers they needed to fill the jobs they had. What does that say about our educational system?

Data from the Alliance for Excellent Education, 2009: 1,800 Vermont dropouts cost the state $459 million of lost lifetime earnings for the state and $19.4 million in health care costs. In other words, what everybody understands is if you don't invest in your young people, they are not going to become productive, tax-paying workers. As often as not, they will get involved in self-destructive activity—drugs, crime, whatever. They will end up in jail, and we end up spending tens of thousands of dollars keeping them in jail rather than seeing them out there as productive members of society contributing their fair share in taxes.

The Urban Institute says we can reduce child poverty— which I mentioned earlier is the highest in the industrialized world—by 35 percent if we provide childcare subsidies to families with income less than 50 percent of a state median.

This is an issue I feel very strongly about. It is, to me, beyond comprehension that in Vermont and throughout this country, it is extremely difficult for working-class families to find affordable, good-quality childcare. We are not back in the 1950s where daddy went to work and mommy stayed home taking care of the kids. Mom is at work as well. And we have families all over this country—middle-class, working-class families—saying, I cannot find quality childcare. We are uncomfortable leaving our two-year-old or three-year-old. We can't find childcare at a rate we can afford.

In this area, again, we are far behind many other countries around the world. Kids who do not get intellectually challenging early childhood education, kids who do not get the emotional support they need from zero to three to four, will enter school already quite behind other kids. Then, years later, 10 years later, they will be dropping out of school and they will be doing drugs and they will be ending up in jail at great expense. How long does it take us to understand that investing in our children, our youngest children, is enormously important for our country? It is a good investment. It is much better to invest in childcare than in keeping people locked up in jails.

Seventy-five percent of American youth who apply to the military are ineligible to serve because of low cognitive capacities, criminal records, or obesity. This is quite unbelievable. Now we are not only talking about not being able to compete internationally because we are not bringing forth the kind of educated people we need, because of the inadequacies of our schools and childcare and so forth—this almost becomes a national security issue, if you like. Seventy-five percent of American youth who apply to the military are ineligible to serve because of low cognitive capacities, criminal records, or obesity. It gives me no pride, no happiness, to bring forth these statistics. But as a nation, we are going to have to grasp these things. Either we can ignore these things, either we can run away from reality, put our heads underneath the carpet, or we can say we are not going to allow America to become a Third World nation, that we are going to turn this country around.

But we are not going to turn the country around unless we rethink our priorities. One of our priorities cannot be more tax breaks for the richest people in this country.

From the 1960s to 2006, the United States fell from first to 18th out of 24 industrialized nations in high school gradua- tion rates. What happens in today's economy if a kid does not graduate high school? If my memory is correct, about 30 percent of our kids—and I know these figures are fuzzy be- cause it is hard to determine who is dropping out and who is not, but my understanding is about 30 percent of our kids drop out of high school. What happens to those kids? Where do they go? How many of them end up in jail? How many of them do drugs? As a nation, I think we can do a lot better than that. We should not have gone from first to 18th out of 24 industrialized nations in high school graduation rates. Dropouts are eight times more likely to be incarcerated. In other words, when kids fail in school, they are going to end up in jail—eight times more likely. Eighty-two percent of those in prison are high school dropouts.

I will tell my colleagues a funny experience. I was in Burlington last week. I met this fellow. He came up and was chatting with me. He said, I just got out of jail. What struck me is he was a well-educated young man. He was very artic- ulate. I suspect he had gone to college. What struck me is how rare that is, as the statistics aptly demonstrate. The people who end up in jail overwhelmingly are high school dropouts, people who don't have the education to make it in the world.

When we talk about the need to substantially increase funding for early childhood education, we should understand that state-funded, pre-K programs currently serve 24 percent of four-year-olds and 4 percent of three-year-olds. In other words, there are millions of families who would like to see their kids be able to access good-quality childcare but can't find that in their states—again, in contrast to giving tax breaks to billionaires who don't need it and in some cases are not even asking for it. The younger the age of investment in human capital, the higher the rate of return on that investment. If society invests early enough, it can raise cognitive and socio-emotional levels and the health of disadvantaged kids. One doesn't need to be a psychologist to understand that. If kids get off to a good start in life, if they have the intellectual support, the intellectual development, and the emotional support, those kids are much more likely to do well in school, much less likely to drop out, much less likely to be a burden on society, much less likely to end up in jail, much less likely to do drugs, et cetera. This is an investment we should be making.

I wish to get back for a moment to the agreement the President made with the Republican leadership and why I think it is a bad agreement and why I believe we can do much better. The way we are going to improve this agreement is when millions of people all over this country say, wait a second. Wait a second. This was an agreement reached behind closed doors. There are Members in the House and the Senate who didn't know about the agreement. What about the average American out there? I wonder how many people believe it makes a lot of sense, with a $13.8 trillion national debt, to be giving huge tax breaks to the wealthiest people in this country?

I have to tell my colleagues, the calls in my office are coming 98, 99 to 1 against these agreements. People think we can do better and our job is to do better. The way we do better is when people all over this country stand up and say, Wait a minute, Congress. Your job is to represent the middle class, to represent our kids, and not to represent the wealthiest people in this country.

I mentioned earlier, I think certainly one of the major objections to this agreement is that it provides tens of billions of dollars to the wealthiest people in this country at a time when the rich are already doing phenomenally well and at a time when the wealthiest people have already experienced huge tax breaks. I think most people think that does not make sense. Let me give an example, not to pick on particular individuals—that is not my goal—but so we know this.

According to the Citizens for Tax Justice, if the Bush tax breaks for the top 2 percent are extended, these are some of the people who will benefit and what kind of benefits they will receive: Rupert Murdoch, the CEO of News Corporation, would receive a $1.3 million tax break next year. Mr. Murdoch is a billionaire. Do we really think he needs that? Jamie Dimon, the head of JPMorgan Chase, whose bank got a $29 billion bailout from the Federal Reserve, will receive a $1.1 million tax break. Trust me, Jamie Dimon, the head of JPMorgan Chase, is doing just fine. Vikram Pandit, the CEO of Citigroup, the bank that got a $50 billion bailout, would receive $785,000 in tax breaks. Ken Lewis, the former CEO of Bank of America—a bank that got a $45 billion bailout—the guy is already fabulously wealthy—would receive a $713,000 tax break. The CEO of Wells Fargo; these are the largest banks in America, the CEOs of these banks are already making huge compensation. John Stumpf, who is the CEO of Wells Fargo, would receive a $318,000 tax break every single year. The CEO of Morgan Stanley, John Mack, whose bank got a $10 billion bailout, would receive a $926,000 a year tax break. The CEO of Aetna, Ronald Williams, would receive a tax break worth $875,000.

I contrast that, as I did earlier, to the fact that two days ago, the Presiding Officer and I and a total of 53 Members of the Senate said, You know, maybe we should provide a $250 check this year to seniors on Social Security and to disabled vets because they haven't gotten a COLA for two years—a $250 check. People making $14,000, $15,000 a year desperately need a little bit of help. We couldn't get one Republican vote. But when it comes to the CEO of a major bank who is already a multimillionaire—we are talking about $6 million, $7 million, $8 million a year in tax breaks—that is not what we should be doing as a nation.

Furthermore, I know President Obama and others have said, Well, let's not worry, because these tax breaks are just temporary—just temporary. They are only going to be given for two years. I have been in Washington long enough to know that when you give a temporary tax break for two years, you are, in fact, giving a long-term tax break or maybe even a permanent tax break. Because two years from now, the exact same arguments will be made: if you do away with those tax breaks for the rich, you are raising taxes. Do you want to raise taxes, a terrible thing to do? That same argument will be made.

But there is one difference. The difference is that when President Obama ran for President and since he has been President, he has time and time again come out against those tax breaks. He does not believe in them. I believe him, and I know that he doesn't. But if he is the Democratic candidate for President and he says: Reelect me to be President because in the future I am going to really get rid of these tax breaks, I am afraid his credibility is not very high because that is what he said last time. I guess there is a limit as to how many times you can cry wolf.

(Mr. LEVIN assumed the Chair.)

Mr. SANDERS. If these tax breaks for the wealthiest people are extended for two years, there is a strong likelihood they will be extended for many years beyond those two and perhaps even permanently. That brings us back to the Bush-era nonsense of believing that tax breaks for the rich and trickle-down economics are going to help the middle-class and working families of this country.

While the personal income tax issue and extending them for the top two percent has received a lot of national attention, what has not gotten a whole lot of discussion is that that is not the only unfair and absurd tax proposal out there.

The agreement struck between the President and the Republican leadership continues the Bush-era 15 percent tax rate on capital gains and dividends, meaning those people who make their living off of their investments will continue to pay a substantially lower tax rate than firemen, teachers, and nurses. So if you are a wealthy person and you earn money from dividends—I believe the overwhelming majority of those dividends accrue to the top 1 percent—you are going to be paying a tax on that income of 15 percent, which is less than you pay if you are a fireman, a police officer, a teacher, or a nurse. So what we are doing there is extending not only the personal income tax breaks for the very rich but a host of other taxes as well.

On top of all of that—and I know many of my colleagues have picked up on this and are extremely upset, and I think that is one of the reasons the Democrats in the House just yesterday said they don't want to bring this proposal to the floor for a vote—this agreement includes a horrendous proposal regarding the estate tax.

The estate tax is a proposal Teddy Roosevelt talked about in the year 1906. It was eventually enacted in 1916. Here is what Teddy Roosevelt said about this issue in August of 1910—and it is worth repeating this because what the proposal struck between the President and the Republican leadership does is lower the estate tax substantially. Here is what Teddy Roosevelt said in 1910: "The absence of effective state, and, especially, national, restraint upon unfair money-getting has tended to create a small class of enormously wealthy and economically powerful men, whose chief object is to hold and increase their power. . . ."

This is Teddy Roosevelt, who by then had served as President of the United States.

He continued: "No man should receive a dollar unless that dollar has been fairly earned. Every dollar received should represent a dollar's worth of service rendered—not gambling in stocks, but service rendered."

This guy was pretty prophetic back in 1910.

He continues: "The really big fortune, the swollen fortune, by the mere fact of its size acquires qualities which differentiate it in kind as well as in degree from what is passed by men of relatively small means. Therefore, I believe in a graduated inheritance tax on big fortunes properly safeguarded against evasion and increasing rapidly in amount with the size of the estate."

Wow, Teddy Roosevelt hit the nail on the head. That was 100 years ago. He was worried that a small group of people with incredible money would be able to pass that money on, and what you would create would be an oligarchic form of government with a small number of people not just holding economic power but significant political power.

It is ironic that, right now, as a result of the disastrous *Citizens United* decision, what Roosevelt foretold, predicted, is exactly what is happening. You have a handful of billionaires now sitting around deciding how much of their fortune they are going to invest in political campaigns all over this country to defeat people like me who are opposed to their agenda and support other people who are in agreement with it. That is what Roosevelt talked about. That is exactly what is happening.

So what we are looking at in this proposal is a situation where the estate tax rate, which was 55 percent under President Clinton with the first $1 million exempted from taxation, will decline to 35 percent, with an exemption on the first $5 million of an individual's estate, $10 million per couple. Here is the important point that has to be made. I think a lot of people don't understand this. Certainly, our Republican friends have done a very good job in distorting reality on this one. There are millions of Americans who believe that when they die, their children will have to pay an estate tax. That is absolutely and categorically incorrect. As this chart shows, only a tiny fraction of estates from deaths in 2009 owed any estate tax. That number is about 0.24 percent. Less than three-tenths of 1 percent of American families paid any tax on the estates they were left. So 99.7 percent of American families did not pay one cent in estate taxes. That is the simple truth. The so-called death tax our Republican friends talk about a whole lot is the estate tax, and 99.7 percent of families don't pay a nickel on it. The people who do pay are not the rich; they are the very, very rich.

Let me give you one example of the absurdity of lowering the estate tax rate or, even worse, ending the estate tax, as some of our Republican colleagues would like to do. If the estate tax was wiped out completely, as Republicans want to do,

Sam Walton's family, the heirs to the Walmart fortune, who are worth about $89 billion. One family is worth $89 billion. They are doing pretty good. If we abolish the estate tax, as our Republican friends would have us do, the Walton family alone would receive an estimated $32.7 billion tax break, if the estate tax was completely repealed—one family, $32.7 billion. This is patently insane. This is insane. Insane.

We have the highest rate of childhood poverty in the industrialized world. We have massive unemployment. I am trying to get seniors—50-plus million people—a $250 check, by the way, because we have not seen a COLA for the last two years for seniors and disabled vets. That would cost, in one year, about $14 billion. The Walton family itself would get more than double in a tax break what some of us are fighting for for over 50 million seniors and disabled vets. We can't afford to give $14 billion to help some of the people in this country who are struggling the hardest. We cannot do that, but somehow we can afford to give $32.7 billion in tax breaks to one of the richest families in this country. If that makes sense to anybody, please call my office. It doesn't make sense to me, and I don't think it makes sense to the vast majority of the American people.

Under this agreement, the estate tax rate, which was 55 percent under President Clinton, with a $1 million tax exemption, will decline to 35 percent, with an exemption on the first $5 million of an individual's estate, $10 million for couples. Let's remember again that this tax applies only to the top three-tenths of 1 percent of the families in this country. This is not just a tax break for the rich; it is a tax break for the very, very rich.

Again, this agreement says we are only going to extend this for two years. Well, frankly, I doubt that very much. I suspect that two years from now the same argument will be made. They will be extending it. Frankly, our Republican colleagues, representing the richest people in the world, are hell-bent on abolishing the estate tax completely.

Those are some of the reasons I think we should be voting against this agreement.

Third—and this is an issue I have been talking about, and I am happy to hear there is more discussion about this in the last few days—is the so-called payroll tax holiday. What that is about is that this would cut $120 billion in Social Security payroll tax for workers. On the surface, this sounds like a very good idea because the worker, instead of paying 6.2 percent into Social Security, pays 4.2 percent. If you think about it for two seconds, you really understand that it is not a good idea because this is money being diverted from the Social Security trust fund.

Social Security, in my view, has been the most successful federal program in perhaps the history of our country. In the last 75 years, whether in good times or bad, Social Security has paid out every nickel owed to every eligible American. Today, Social Security has a $2.6 trillion surplus. Today, Social Security can pay out benefits for the next 27 years. Our goal, and what we must do, is make sure we extend it beyond 27 years, for the next 75 years. Well, if we divert $120 billion from the Social Security trust fund and give it to workers today, what you are doing is cutting back the viability—the long-term viability—of Social Security.

That is not just Bernie Sanders raising this issue. There are many people representing millions of senior citizens who are deeply concerned about this proposal—this provision in the agreement between the President and the Republican leadership.

The National Committee to Preserve Social Security and Medicare is one of the very largest senior groups in America. They do a very good job. We have many seniors in Vermont who are members of this organization. Their job is to do what the title of the organization suggests, which is to preserve Social Security and Medicare. Just the other day, they sent out a news release, and the title of the news release was "Cutting Contributions to Social Security Signals the Beginning of the End; Payroll Tax Holiday is Anything But."

Let me quote from Barbara Kennelly, a former member of Congress, who is the president and CEO of the National Committee to Preserve Social Security and Medicare:

"Even though Social Security contributed nothing to the current economic crisis, it has been bartered in a deal that provides deficit-busting tax cuts for the wealthy. Diverting $120 billion in Social Security contributions for a so-called 'tax holiday' may sound like a good deal for workers now, but it is bad business for the program that a majority of middle-class seniors will rely upon in the future."

That, again, is a quote from Barbara Kennelly, President and CEO of the National Committee to Preserve Social Security and Medicare.

Mr. President, I think many of us should understand where this concept originated. This is not a progressive idea. This is an idea that came from Republicans and conservatives who want to end Social Security. I want to read an interesting quote from a gentleman named Bruce Bartlett. Mr. Bartlett was a former top adviser to Presidents Reagan and George H.W. Bush. This is what he wrote in opposition to this payroll tax cut:

"What are the odds that Republicans will ever allow this one-year tax holiday to expire? They wrote the Bush tax cuts with explicit expiration dates, and then when it came time for the law they wrote to take effect exactly as they wrote it, they said any failure to extend them permanently would constitute the biggest tax increase in history."

So what Mr. Bartlett is saying—and I will go back to his quote in a second—is what we all know to be true: that around here, in Congress, if you provide a tax break for one year—in this case a payroll tax holiday—a year from now, if you restore the old rates—which are 6.2 percent—our Republican friends are going to say Democrats are raising your taxes. It ain't gonna happen.

This one-year extension could well become a permanent extension, and if it becomes a permanent extension, you are diverting a huge amount of money from Social Security and you are weakening the entire financial structure of Social

Security in this country, which I expect is exactly what some would like to do.

President Obama says: Well, not to worry. It is only one year. Don't worry, that one year is going to be covered by the Federal Government.

So for the very first time, out of the Treasury Department, money is going to come into Social Security, which has always been 100 percent dependent, as it should be, on payroll taxes. For the first time, we are breaking that. Around here you do it once and it is going to continue.

Barbara Kennelly, the President of the National Committee to Preserve Social Security and Medicare, says: "Cutting these contributions to Social Security signals the beginning of the end."

So we should be very, very, very mindful of that. We should not support this payroll tax holiday. It is one of the more dangerous provisions in this agreement.

But let me get back now, if I might, to what Bruce Bartlett—a former top adviser for Presidents Reagan and George H.W. Bush—recently wrote:

"If allowing the Bush tax cuts to expire is the biggest tax increase in history—one that Republicans claim would decimate a still fragile economy—then surely the expiration of a payroll tax holiday would also constitute a massive tax increase on the working people of America. Republicans would prefer to destroy Social Security's finances or permanently fund it with general revenues than allow a once-suspended payroll tax to be reimposed. Arch Social Security hater Peter

Ferrara once told me that funding it with general revenues was part of his plan to destroy it by converting Social Security into a welfare program rather than an earned benefit."

Once again, that is a quote from Bruce Bartlett, a former adviser to President Reagan and the first President Bush. So what he is saying is—and this is maybe one of the sleeping issues in this agreement between the President and the Republican leadership—we may be taking a huge step forward in destroying the most important program in this country—which is Social Security—by diverting now $120 billion, and in the future hundreds and hundreds of billions of dollars from this program so that, in fact, it will not be there for our kids and our grandchildren.

Mr. President, the fourth point I want to make in opposition to this agreement—and one that I have made before and read a little bit about—is that while some of the business taxes in this agreement may work to create jobs, some of them won't. The more important point is that economists on both ends of the political spectrum believe the better way to spur the economy and to create the millions and millions of jobs we must create is to rebuild our crumbling infrastructure.

Just a few minutes ago I read excerpts from a very good book by a friend of mine, Arianna Huffington, entitled *Third World America*. The purpose of her book was to give us a warning that if we as a nation do not get our act together in a variety of ways, including our physical infrastructure, we are headed down the pike to be a Third World nation.

According to the American Society of Civil Engineers, we as a nation need to spend $2.2 trillion in the next five years alone in order to take care of our infrastructure needs.

Unfortunately, this agreement, signed by the President and the Republicans, doesn't put one penny into infrastructure. So if we are serious about creating jobs, if we are serious about making sure our economy can be competitive in the global economy, we have to be watching what other countries are doing, and they are investing far more than we are.

The stimulus package, by the way, will help us very much in Vermont in this area. Right now, if you were to drive around the State of Vermont—and I think in many other places in this country—and you took out your cell phone, you would find it very hard to make calls in a number of areas of the state. A few months ago, I was literally a mile and a half away from our state capital in Montpelier, near Northfield, Vermont. I could not make a telephone call with my cell phone. That is true in many parts of Vermont and in many areas of America. We are lagging behind many other countries in terms of the accessibility of cell phone service and broadband—and broadband.

So I am happy to say that in Vermont we received a very generous grant through the stimulus package that will help us, and other states received similar grants. But those are areas where we have to invest. You have to invest in broadband and make sure cell phone service is available in rural America—all over America. I talked a moment ago about our train services. There are train services today which are worse than they were

30 or 40 years ago. It takes longer to get from destination A to destination B. China is investing huge sums of money building high-speed rail at a rate that we could not even dream about.

So while in this agreement we do have money for business tax cuts, I do not think that is the best way to invest taxpayer money if we are serious about creating the jobs that we need. Corporate America already is sitting on close to $2 trillion cash on hand. I don't know that more tax breaks are going to help them very much. I think that it is a lot smarter—and I think most economists agree with me—to be investing in our infrastructure, both to create jobs now and to improve our competitiveness in years to come.

Further, Mr. President, I want to say a word on this—I mentioned this earlier today: President Obama talks about this being a compromise agreement, that you can't get everything you want. I certainly understand that. But one of the aspects of the compromise he points to is an extension of unemployment benefits for 13 months. Well, let me be very clear. I think at a time when 2 million of our fellow Americans are about to lose their unemployment, at a time when unemployment is extraordinarily high—long-term unemployment is, I think, higher than at any point on record, with people looking for work month after month after month and not finding it—it would be morally unacceptable if this country did not extend unemployment benefits for those workers for 13 months. Yet the President sees this as a great sign of compromise.

I would argue the contrary. I would suggest to you that for the past 40 years, under both Democratic and Republican administrations and under Democratic and Republican leadership in the Senate or in the House, whenever the unemployment rate has been above 7.2 percent, unemployment insurance has always been extended. In other words, this has been a bipartisan policy for 40 years. I don't want to see us accepting as a really great give on the part of Republicans—something that they are giving us as part of a compromise—when it has been bipartisan policy for 40 years under Democratic and Republican leadership. So I don't accept this as a great gift. I think the American people understand you don't turn your backs on unemployed workers—people who have been unemployed for long periods of time. You don't allow those people to lose their homes. You don't force these people out into the streets. You don't take away what shreds of dignity they have remaining. That is not what you do. That has always been Republican philosophy as well as Democratic philosophy. This is not a great gift. So I do not accept this is a compromise.

Let me be very clear. As I said earlier, I do believe there are positive parts of this agreement that must be maintained as we move forward toward a better agreement. Let me cite some of them that make a lot of sense to me and that I believe we have to retain and build on.

The obvious one, in addition to extending unemployment benefits, is we have to extend middle-class tax cuts for 98 percent of working Americans. As I have been documenting over and over again today, we are looking at a situation where the middle class in this country is collapsing. Under President

Bush, the median family income went down by $2,200. People are losing their health care. It would be asinine, it would be unacceptable if the middle class did not continue to receive the tax breaks that were developed in 2001 and 2003. That, to a large degree, is what this fight is about. We have to extend those tax breaks to the middle class but not tax breaks to the millionaires and billionaires.

Further, there are some other good provisions in this agreement—the earned-income tax credit for working Americans and the child and college tax credits—and they are very important. They will keep millions of our fellow Americans from slipping out of the middle class and into poverty, and they will allow millions of our fellow citizens to send their kids to college.

I just talked a moment ago about the fact that we have over 100,000 families in this country where kids graduate high school wanting to go to college but can't afford to do so. This proposal will help them do that, and that is right.

But despite the fact there are some good and important provisions in this proposal, when we look at the overall package, when we look at a $13.8 trillion national debt and a declining middle class, I think what we have to say is this package just doesn't do it. It is just not good enough.

The President says he knows how to count votes. I understand that. He says: Well, you had a couple of votes here to make sure that we would not give tax breaks to millionaires. And the President has been very clear he does not want to do that. I understand that. But he says: What choice do I have?

I think the answer is that we have to fight this issue. In my view, the solution ultimately will not be resolved inside the Beltway, in the Senate or in the House. It will be resolved when millions of Americans get on their telephones, get on their computers, and let their Senators and their Members of the House of Representatives know they are profoundly outraged that at a time when the rich never had it so good, and when we have a huge national debt, this agreement contains huge tax breaks for those people who don't need it. That is how we defeat this.

I am not sure that all alone here in the debate I am going to turn any of my Republican or even some Democratic colleagues around.

But I do believe that, if people all over this country stand up and say: Wait a minute, how much do the richest people in this country want? I just documented a few moments ago that the top 400 wealthiest people in this country saw a doubling of their income under President Bush—a doubling of their income—and tax rates went down. When is enough enough? How much do they need?

I think and I would hope, by the way, that this is certainly not just a progressive issue. I am a progressive. This is a conservative issue. Year after year, I have heard our conservative friends telling us: My goodness, we just cannot continue to raise the national debt; we have to do something about this unsustainable deficit. This agreement grows, increases the national debt. What kind of honest conservative can vote to increase the national debt? And if they do, please, no more lectures here on the floor of the Senate. Your hypocrisy will be known to everybody. Don't tell us you are concerned about the national debt and give tax breaks to billionaires and raise the national debt so our kids and grandchildren in the middle class will have to pay higher taxes in order to pay off the debt that was caused by you giving tax breaks to millionaires. Please, no more lectures on that issue. Just say: OK, rich people contributed to my campaign; I have to do what they want. That will be honest. Please, no more lectures about your concern about the national debt.

Again, I want to reiterate this point. Everybody says: Don't worry, these are only two years. These are not, in my view, two years. If you do them for two years, the same old argument will be back two years from now, and we will be in the midst of a Presidential election. What our Republican friends will say, as sure as I am standing here—and I am glad we have a gentleman putting this in the *Congressional Record*. I want people to go back to the *Congressional Record*. I am sure I will be proven right that two years from now our Republican friends will come back and they will say: Oh, my word, if you repeal these tax breaks, you are going to be raising taxes. We can't do that.

What will make the situation even more difficult two years from now than today is you have President Obama—if he is the Democratic candidate two years from now, he will say: I don't believe in these tax breaks for the rich, and I will do my best to repeal them. But his credibility has been damaged because that is what he said in the last campaign. That is what he has been saying all along. The President does not believe in extending these tax breaks for the wealthy. I know that. Everybody knows that. But if he caves in now, who is going to believe he is not going to do the same thing two years from now? That is the damage.

Then I think what is even more troublesome is that once we move down the path of more tax breaks for the very wealthy, we are accepting the heart and soul of trickle-down economics, which has been, to my mind, a proven disaster, a failure. I remind the listeners and my colleagues that these tax breaks have been in existence since 2001. They were in existence throughout almost all of President Bush's tenure. The end result was that we lost over 600,000 private sector jobs—lost over 600,000 private sector jobs, the worst job performance record maybe in the history of this country. Trickle-down economics does not work.

Giving tax breaks to billionaires does not stimulate the economy. Helping working families and the middle class get decent jobs and tax breaks for people who need the money and are going to spend the money is what creates jobs, not giving tax breaks to billionaires who do not need it and who are not going to spend it.

Again, the point I want to make here is that if people think, oh, this is just temporary, this is just two years, I believe they are kidding themselves. I believe that two years from now, the debate will be about extending them or perhaps even making them permanent.

At a time, as I mentioned earlier, where the top 1 percent has seen a huge increase in the percentage of income they earn in this country—going from 8 percent in the 1970s to 23.5 percent in 2007—and where the top 1 percent now earns more income than the bottom 50 percent, it is totally absurd to be giving tax breaks to people who do not need them, and it is not good economics, as well.

Here is the other irony, as I also mentioned earlier—I guess by this time, I am going to be doing a little repetition here. But as I mentioned earlier, you have a number of millionaires and some of the richest people in this country who will benefit from these tax breaks. Do you know what they are saying? Do you know what Warren Buffett is saying? Do you know what Bill Gates is saying? Do you know what Ben Cohen from Ben & Jerry's is saying? Do you know what many other wealthy people are saying? Hey, thanks very much; I don't need it. It is more important that you invest in our children. It is more important that we protect working families. We are doing just fine, thanks. Our incomes have soared, our tax rates have gone down, and we don't need it. In other words, we have this absurd situation that not only is this bad public policy, we are actually forcing tax breaks on people who don't need them and don't even want them. The richest people in this country—Bill Gates, Warren Buffett—don't want it.

Here is something else. Here is something else that needs to be understood. What the Republicans are doing in this agreement is driving up the national debt. You may think that is not what the Republicans really believe in. They are supposed to be conservatives. They don't want a high national debt. Why would they be giving tax breaks to the rich and driving up the national debt? There is a rationale. These guys are not dumb, and I think they know what they are doing. Here is what the argument is. If you drive up the national debt and the deficit, you then come back to the floor of the Senate and you say: You know what, this national debt and deficit is unsustainable. The only way we can deal with it now is by cutting, cutting, cutting. We are already beginning to hear how some of those thoughts are going to develop.

There was, as you know, a deficit reduction commission appointed by the President. When I heard who was going to be chairing that commission and cochairing it—Alan Simpson, a very nice gentleman but a very conservative gentleman who has attacked Social Security for a very long period of time, and Erskine Bowles, a conservative Democrat—I had serious doubts about what was going to come out of that commission. The good news is, they needed 14 votes to pass their recommendations and they didn't get the 14. But a lot of the ideas that Senator *Simpson* and Mr. Bowles developed are going to be filtering around this institution.

What the Republicans will say is that when you have a huge debt—which they helped create—we are going to have to cut. What are we going to have to do? As you recall, that deficit reduction commission recommended a savage cut—over 20 percent—in Social Security benefits for young workers—major cuts. There was talk about raising the Social Security age up to 69. They are talking about cuts in Medicare, cuts in Medicaid, cuts in education.

Right now—I think I have documented it a dozen times—it is a horrendous situation when so many of our young people cannot afford to go to college, and the others who do go to college and graduate end up on average $24,000 in debt. These guys on the deficit reduction commission were recommending that the interest on that debt be accrued while students are in college.

Here we have us slipping behind the rest of the world in terms of our percentage of college graduates, and this recommendation is on young people, who do not have a lot of money, who are borrowing money, that they will have to pay more to go to college. You are going to see it.

Here is the argument—good, it is going to be in the *Congressional Record*. Check it out, see if I am right. The argument will be: The deficit is going up, the national debt is going up. We have to attack and cut Social Security, Medicare, Medicaid, veterans programs.

This year—Senator *Landrieu* from Louisiana made this point a little while ago—and I think this is roughly right—our soldiers, men and women in the Armed Forces, are going to get a 1.4 percent increase in their salaries this year, 1.4 percent for people putting their lives on the line to defend this country. A $250 check for 50-plus million seniors and disabled vets—we couldn't pass it; too much money—$14 billion.

They are going to come back and cut and cut in the name of trying to deal with the high deficit which they are now increasing. That is an issue we must be addressing.

In my view, while there are some good parts of the proposal, it is certainly one that should be significantly improved. I believe the way it can be improved is by the American people beginning to get involved in the process.

I can tell you, as I said earlier, I don't know how the calls are going today in my office because I have been here, but for the last three days, we have received thousands of phone calls and e-mails, and over 98 percent of them have been against this proposal. The American people believe, the people in Vermont believe we can do a lot better job in crafting a proposal that represents the middle class and our kids and not just the wealthiest people in this country.

When we talk about this proposal negotiated by the White House and Republican leadership, again, it has to be put within the broad context of what is going on in America. That context is not a pretty picture. That context requires us to understand that the middle class, which has been the backbone of this country for so very long, is in the process of disappearing. That context makes us understand that millions of families in this country are worried, parents are worried, not just about their own lives—they are prepared to work 50 or 60 hours a week; they are prepared to cut back on their own needs. I think what is hurting them more deeply is the kind of future they are contemplating for their children. They are worried that, for the first time in the modern history of America, their kids will get jobs that will pay them lower salaries than what the parents have earned. They are worried that unemployment will be much more likely for their kids than for themselves. They are worried that while they were able to scrape through—in my case, I was able to scrape through college. I borrowed some money, did some jobs, and made it like millions of other people. They are worried that with the high cost of a college education and the reduction in their real earnings, they are not going to be able to send their kids to college. I have received e-mails—and I am sure you have, Mr. President—the saddest thing in the world, where you have parents who are saying: We have saved all of our lives for the thing we wanted the most, which was to be able to send our son or daughter to college, and we can't do that now. That is the overall context this agreement has to be placed within.

The issue is, again and again, the richest people in this country do not need tax breaks. They are doing phenomenally well. They have already been given huge amounts of tax breaks. It is the middle class, it is the working families, it is the lower income people we have to be worrying about and not just the wealthy and the powerful.

When we talk about why the middle class is declining, that is a tough issue. I am not here to suggest I know all of the answers. I surely don't. It is a complicated issue. Honest people have differences of opinion. But let me touch on a few areas that I think will explain why poverty is going up and the middle class is going down. One of them deals with our trade policies.

I can remember a number of years ago I was in the House of Representatives, and I can remember the lobbyists and the big money interests coming around and saying: If you guys would only pass NAFTA, this would create a whole lot of jobs in the United States because we would be able to ship products made in America to Mexico. In fact, as I recall—it seems almost humorous now—what they said is: If we pass NAFTA, it would solve the problem of illegal immigration because the economy of Mexico would be so strong that people would stay in their own country and not try to sneak across the border. That is, as we look back on it, somewhat humorous, that that issue was even discussed.

But one of the areas that, unfortunately, for a variety of reasons, we have not dealt with is our disastrous trade policy. That is NAFTA; that is permanent Normal Trade Relations with China; that is trade policies which have encouraged large corporations in this country to send jobs abroad because they can find workers in other countries, in low-wage countries, who are prepared to work for pennies an hour.

I think not only have we not addressed this issue from an economic perspective the way we should, I have to tell you, I know that during campaigns, a lot of Members of Congress put their 30-second ads on the air saying how concerned they are about outsourcing and our trade policy. But somehow, the day after the election, I didn't hear that discussion resume on the floor of the House or the Senate. I want to say this is true not just of Republicans but of Democrats as well.

A lot of Democrats campaign on the need for trade reform, but it does not happen. In fact, I have been here in the Senate now for almost four years. I have not heard one serious—underline "serious"—discussion to explain how in recent years we have lost millions and millions of manufacturing jobs, when those jobs were the backbone of the working class of this country, providing not only decent wages but decent benefits, decent health care, decent pensions.

There was once a time in this country when a manufacturing job was a ticket to the middle class. I have to say something because I remember not so many years ago, there were national leaders saying: Well—to the young people—you do not have to worry about that factory work anymore. You do not have to be involved in production because, you know what. All of the jobs in the future are going to be nice and clean in offices and on computers.

I think we demeaned and insulted the people who built the products we consumed. There is nothing wrong with a factory job if workers there earn a decent wage and have a decent benefit. Those are the jobs that built America. I remember, and we should never forget—and we now have celebrated the anniversary of Pearl Harbor. There was a speech that President Roosevelt gave a day after Pearl Harbor, in a joint session to the Congress, when he declared war on Japan.

I saw a video of that speech. It was a remarkable speech because, at that moment, at that moment, the United States was not only fighting Japan, and we knew the fight with Germany and Nazism was right around the corner, at that point we were having to fight a war on two fronts: in Asia and in Europe. Hitler was on the march; the Japanese were in China. The Japanese had just attacked Pearl Harbor. Here we were, just about to enter the war. How could we possibly win that war?

Yet because of the manufacturing capabilities that we had at that time, and this is an amazing story, literally in two and a half years the war was essentially won, obviously not completed until 1945. But because of the incredible industrial capabilities in this country, the ability to transform our manufacturing sector from a consumer-oriented sector, from automobiles into tanks; from shirts into uniforms; from hunting rifles into machine guns, within two or three years we had essentially won that war. It was an incredible effort on the part of workers in this country who transformed our economy into an industrial force that was able to supply our soldiers with the weapons that they needed to defeat Hitler and the Japanese.

Where are we today in terms of our manufacturing capabilities? As I mentioned earlier, a couple of weeks ago, my wife and I went shopping for Christmas presents, in just a plain old department store. It is literally very hard to find a product not manufactured in China. It is very hard to find a product, a gift that we could buy that was manufactured in the United States of America.

I think people understand instinctively that this country will not be a major economic player in years to come if we allow our manufacturing base to continue to decline. Again, just under Bush, we went from about 17 million manufacturing jobs down to roughly 12 million jobs, in eight years of Bush. How do we survive as a strong industrial power if our manufacturing jobs disappear?

Today there are fewer manufacturing jobs in this country than there were in April of 1941, about eight months before the attack on Pearl Harbor; fewer manufacturing jobs today than in April of 1941. Those manufacturing jobs that are left—that are left—in many cases pay lower wages, with fewer benefits, than they did a generation ago.

In other words, we are moving not only in a decline in our manufacturing jobs but in the wages our workers earn and the benefits they receive.

I raise all of these issues to put this agreement between the President and the Republican leadership in a broader context. Today—and this is just an incredible fact, and it is absolutely frightening to the future of the middle class in this country—today, entry level automobile workers at General Motors and Chrysler now earn half as much, half as much as their peers made just one year ago. Instead of making $28 an hour, a middle-class wage, they are now making $14 an hour. This is in the automobile industry which has always been the gold standard for manufacturing jobs in America. If workers with a union in the automobile industry are making $14 an hour, what do you think workers in New Mexico are going to be making without a strong union?

So what you are seeing is a dissolution of the middle class, wages are going down, and in this remarkable example, a

50 percent reduction; the older workers making good wages, new workers half the wages.

Is this the future of America? Is this what our kids have to look forward to, that they are going to be earning half the wages their fathers made, that their mothers made? Is that the future? In the midst of all of that, we run up a huge national debt, send our jobs to China, and we give tax breaks to millionaires? Is that the future these kids have to look forward to? I certainly hope not. We are going to have to be tough, and we are going to have to take on some very powerful special interests to turn this whole thing around.

Today I have devoted a lot of time to our national debt, $13.8 trillion, and to our deficit, which is $1.3 trillion. But we cannot ignore our trade deficit. In 2008, our trade deficit was nearly $700 billion. Last year our trade deficit with China alone was almost $227 billion. In other words, we are purchasing a whole lot more products than we are selling.

Sometimes I get a kick out of hearing the defenders of our trade policy talk about all of the products we are exporting. Well, yeah, we are exporting a lot, but we are importing a heck of a lot more. So I think what you have is a major economic issue. That economic issue is that we are losing millions of good-paying jobs because of our disastrous trade policy. Furthermore, the jobs we have, on those jobs, we are seeing a decline in wages and in benefits.

I think the bottom line of this is not just an economic issue, it is a moral issue as well, and that is when companies such as General Electric and all the rest—I do not mean to be picking a lot on General Electric, but I have a quote I want to read. This was a few years back. I think it is important because it applies not just to General Electric. But I want people to hear this. GE is, of course, one of our major corporations. The Federal Reserve's recent disclosure pointed out, the taxpayers of this country, through the Fed, provided a $16 billion bailout to General Electric during the recent crisis. This is what the head, the CEO of General Electric, Jeffrey Immelt, said in 2002, December 6:

"When I am talking to GE managers, I talk China, China, China, China, China. You need to be there. You need to change the way people talk about it and how they get there. I am a nut on China. Outsourcing from China is going to grow to $5 billion. We are building a tech center in China. Every discussion today has to center on China. The cost basis is extremely attractive. You can take an 18-cubic-foot refrigerator, make it in China, land it in the United States, and land it for less than we can make an 18-cubic-foot refrigerator today ourselves."

Gee. A couple of years ago when GE had some difficult economic times, and they needed $16 billion to bail them out, I did not hear Mr. Immelt going to China, China, China, China, China. I did not hear that. I heard Mr. Immelt going to the taxpayers of the United States for his welfare check.

So I say to Mr. Immelt, and I say to all of those CEOs who have been so quick to run to China, that maybe it is time to start reinvesting in the United States of America. But it is not just Mr. Immelt. I do not mean to just pick on him. It is all of them. They all see the future in China, in Vietnam, in countries where people work for pennies an hour.

Mr. Immelt came to his decision in the footsteps of the former CEO of GE, Jack Welch. What Jack Welch was famously quoted as saying:

"Ideally," said the guy who was head of General Electric before Immelt, "Ideally, we would have every plant we own on a barge."

Do you remember that quote? He said: "Ideally, we would have every plant we own on a barge."

What did he mean by that? What he meant by that, if you are on a barge, you can move your plant to any part of the world where the labor is cheapest. So if it gets too expensive in China, and you have to pay people 75 cents an hour, you go to Vietnam. If it gets too expensive in Vietnam, maybe you can go to North Korea and have people work under martial law. I do not know.

But what he was saying is, his goal was to make sure that GE would create jobs in those countries in the world where workers were paid the lowest possible wage.

Former GE executive vice president Frank Doyle said:

"We did a lot of violence to the expectations of the American workforce. We downsized, we delayered, and we outsourced."

He was honest enough to admit that. But, again, I do not mean to just pick on Jeff Immelt or General Electric. It is a history of corporations all over America.

Let me just mention that the CEO of Cisco, John Chambers—and this is what he says. You know, we tell the young people: The future is in information technology. We want you guys to be smart. Learn how to use computers. You are not going to work in factories.

This is what the CEO of Cisco, certainly one of the large IT companies in the United States, said: "China will become the IT center of the world. And we can have a healthy discussion about whether that's in 2020 or 2040. What we are trying to do is outline an entire strategy of becoming a Chinese company."

This was in 2004.

Furthermore—

He says, October 15, 2004—this is from the CEO of Cisco: "We believe in giving something back and truly becoming a Chinese company."

Meanwhile, when Cisco needs tax breaks, they get it from the taxpayers of the United States of America. Boy, are they taking us for dummies. They outsource their jobs to China and we give them tax breaks.

In the last campaign, one of the folks who ended up getting a lot more publicity than he usually does is the president and CEO of the U.S. Chamber of Commerce, a gentleman named Tom Donohue.

(Mr. UDALL of New Mexico assumed the chair.)

Mr. SANDERS. Again, my point is not to just pick on individuals. Every quote I am giving can be multiplied 50, 100 times over. This is what corporate America believes. They believe it is totally appropriate to throw American workers out on the street, move to low-wage countries, China and other countries, pay people a few cents an hour, and bring their products back into the United States.

Mr. Tom Donohue is the president and CEO of the U.S. Chamber of Commerce. He got a lot of publicity during the last election because the Chamber of Commerce became the funnel for a lot of money that went into campaigns around the country. They raised tens of millions of dollars, a lot of the money was undisclosed. All the rich folks and billionaires gave money to the Chamber of Commerce, and they were able to elect candidates who were sympathetic to their point of view.

Let's find out what their point of view is. This is a quote Mr. Donohue made going back to 2004: "One job sent overseas, if it happens to be my job, is one too many. But the benefits of offshoring jobs outweighs the cost."

That was Tom Donohue, president and CEO of the largest business organization in America. They are in favor of offshoring American jobs. They think it is a good idea. They understand that if corporations throw American workers out on the street and go to China and pay people there pennies an hour, it will make more profits. Give them credit. They are upfront about it. We don't care about the United States of America. We don't care about young people. We don't care about the future of this country. The future of the world is in China.

Here is a quote that appeared in The Associated Press on July 1, 2004:

"U.S. Chamber of Commerce President and CEO Thomas Donohue urged American companies to send jobs overseas."

That was in 2004. This is an AP story.

"U.S. Chamber of Commerce President and CEO Thomas Donohue."

This is the head of the largest business organization in America. That is where all these businesses come together to develop policy, to lobby us, to provide campaign contributions—"urged American companies to send jobs overseas."

That is really patriotic. That is standing up for the United States.

"Donohue said Wednesday that exporting high-paid tech jobs to low-cost countries such as India, China, and Russia saves companies money." It's no surprise that Donohue, who tripled the Chamber of Commerce's lobbying team since 1997 and aggressively promotes pro-business policies, endorses offshoring. The 3 million member organization, the Chamber of Commerce, the world's largest business consortium, champions tax cuts, free trade, workers compensation reform, and more liberal trade policies with China.

What more do we need to understand why we have lost millions of good-paying manufacturing jobs, why wages are going down? What more do we need when the president of the Chamber of Commerce tells us he thinks it is good public policy to send jobs to China? I don't think there is much we have to discover. They are telling us this.

In a moment what I will be talking about is how these ideas from the big-moneyed people become implemented in

policy which is shaped by lobbying and campaign contributions. Before I go there, I wish to give some more examples
about how business leaders feel about the workers of this
country and its young people.

This, again, is a quote. I apologize. It is a few years old,
from 2004, January 19. This is from Alan Lacy, the CEO of
Sears Roebuck and Company at the time:

"There are four or five times as many smart, driven people
in China than there are in the United States. And there are another four or five, three or four times as many people in India
that are smarter or as smart or have more drive. And if technology is now going to basically reduce location as a barrier
to competition"—i.e., you have a World Wide Web and you
can do your work in China or India—"then essentially you
have something like, whatever that was, seven or nine times
more smart, committed people than are now competing in
this marketplace against certain activities. So we are going
to see, I think, a huge incentive to ship some of these more
commodity-like knowledge workers' jobs offshore."

So here we have our blue-collar jobs decimated, and we
told the kids not to worry. You didn't want to work in the
factory anyhow. We have good information technology,
computer-based jobs for you. But then you have the heads of
large corporations saying: Why do I want American young
people to do this? I can have Indian young people do it who
will work for a fraction of the wages. We all see this. It is
nothing new. You try to get a plane reservation and you are
talking to somebody in India. Please, do not hear me as being

anti-Indian or anti-Chinese. That is the furthest thing I would want anyone to think. We want to work with people all over the world. But we don't have to destroy the middle class of this country to help people around the world. You don't have to be a corporate CEO to sell out your own people who built your company to run abroad. This Senator is not anti-Chinese, far from it, I am not anti-Indian, anti-Vietnamese. I guess I plead guilty to being pro-American. Maybe that is suspect here.

The former CEO of Hewlett-Packard, Carly Fiorina, ran for Senator. This is what she said when she was the CEO of Hewlett-Packard in 2004: "There is no job that is America's God-given right anymore."

I could go on and on and on, but I think we have the point. The point is that when things get rough for corporate America, as they did recently for General Electric, they run to the taxpayers in order to be bailed out. But their overall philosophy is that their goal in life is to make as much money as they can in any way they can, and, therefore, you run to those countries where wages are low.

We are seeing it all the time. It is not just blue collar; it is increasingly white collar. We have radiologists who are reading X-rays in India. People behind the computer can do work in India as well as here, and these corporate folks have taken advantage of that and sold out the young people of this country and the working class.

It is virtually impossible to find anything in a Walmart or other stores such as that that is made in America today. This is essentially true for clothing. An increasing amount of clothing comes from Bangladesh. Today, there are 4,000 garment factories in Bangladesh making clothing for Walmart, Gap, JC Penney, Levi Strauss, Tommy Hilfiger, and many others. Garment workers in Bangladesh, some 3.5 million of them—and the number is growing—are among the lowest paid workers in the world. They have difficulty buying enough food and shelter for their own needs.

The good news is the minimum wage in Bangladesh was doubled. It went from 11.5 cents an hour to 22 cents an hour. So when you buy your shirt made in Bangladesh, you have young women there coming in from the countryside who are now paid, because of a doubling of the minimum wage, 22 cents an hour. Is that something our people should be asked to compete against? Should we say to the American worker: We can get you jobs. We are prepared to invest in the United States. We are an American company. You helped make us great. Thank you for the work you have done over the years. Thank you for purchasing our products. Thank you for making us strong. If you are prepared to work for $1 an hour, $2 an hour, $3 an hour, we will come back.

By the way, in the last campaign, what did we hear rumblings of? Abolishing the minimum wage. The minimum wage is now $7.25 an hour. There are people out there who say: Look, if I can hire somebody in China for $2 or $3 an hour and you want a job in America and I have to pay you $7.25 an hour, why would I want to do that? If we abolish the minimum wage, I may hire you.

What a wonderful prospect for our young people to think about, working for $4 or $5 an hour.

If we want to understand why the middle class is collapsing, why unemployment is high, why our manufacturing base has been decimated, why it is hard to purchase a product made in the United States, it has a lot to do with our trade policies, which were pushed by people such as Mr. Donohue of the Chamber of Commerce and many others.

But it is not just a disastrous trade policy that has brought us to where we are today. The immediate cause of this crisis is—and this gets me sick thinking about it—what the crooks on Wall Street have done to the American people. These people fought for a period of years to deregulate the banking industry. These people said to us: Well, if you just would do away with Glass-Steagall, if you will just allow financial institutions, commercial banks, investment banks, insurance companies, if you allow them to merge, do away with these walls which Glass-Steagall, since the Great Depression, established, my God, it will be just terrific. It will be good for the economy, good for the American people, good for our international competitiveness.

I remember those debates because I was at that point in the House of Representatives. I was a member of the Financial Services Committee at that point. I was on the committee that dealt with that. I remember all the times Alan Greenspan came before the committee and Robert Rubin. We had Republicans, Democrats coming before the committee and saying: This is what you have to do. You have to deregulate. You have to let these guys merge. Bigger is better. Against my votes. Somewhere on the Internet there is a discussion I had with Alan Greenspan when he came before our committee. I made it very clear to the people of Vermont, to him and everybody else, that I did not think deregulation was a good idea, that I thought it would lead to disaster. Someplace in this world there is a quote of mine which pretty much predicts what was going to happen. But needless to say, I was one vote. The majority of the Members in the House and Senate voted to deregulate. The rest is, unfortunately, history.

What we saw is people on Wall Street operating from a business model based on fraud, based on dishonesty, understanding that the likelihood of them ever getting caught was small, that if things got very bad, they would be bailed out by the taxpayers, understanding that they are too powerful to ever be put in jail, to be indicted, understanding that in this country when you are a CEO on Wall Street, you have so much wealth and so much power and so many lawyers and so many friends in Congress, you could do pretty much anything you want and not much is going to happen to you—and they did it. Their greed and recklessness and their illegal behavior destroyed this economy.

What they did to the American people is so horrible. Here we had a middle class which was already being battered as a result of trade agreements, loss of manufacturing jobs, health care costs going up, couldn't afford to send their children to college—that had gone on for years—and then these guys started pushing worthless and complicated financial instruments and the whole thing explodes.

And they come crying to the taxpayers of America to bail them out.

I will never forget—never forget—Hank Paulson coming before the Democratic caucus—I am an Independent and have long been serving as an Independent in Congress—saying that within a few days he needed $700 billion or the entire world's financial system would collapse. My suggestion to him at that meeting was: If you need the money, why don't you go to your friends and get the money? Why don't you go to all your banker friends and millionaire friends and billionaire friends and get some of that money, and don't go to the middle class of this country that has already been harmed.

In fact, we brought an amendment to the floor of the Senate, which was one of the first amendments I brought as a Senator, which said that millionaires and billionaires should pay for the bailout, not the American people. It got defeated on a voice vote.

So what happens on Wall Street is we have seen a tremendous concentration of ownership there, another issue we do not talk enough about. I know Senator *Brown* and Senator *Kaufman* and I worked on a proposal to try to break up these large financial institutions. I think we got 30-some-odd votes on that. We could not do it.

So what the American people should know now is, while we bailed out Wall Street, because they were too big to fail, three out of the four largest financial institutions—all of whom were bailed out very significantly—are now larger today than they were before the bailout.

Incredibly, since the start of the financial crisis, Wells Fargo has grown 43 percent bigger, JPMorgan Chase has grown 51 percent bigger, and Bank of America is now 138 percent larger than before the financial crisis began.

Can you imagine that? We bailed these guys out because they were too big to fail, and now three out of the four largest ones are much larger than they were. How did that happen? Well, in 2008, Bank of America—the largest commercial bank in this country—which received a $45 billion taxpayer bailout from the Treasury Department, purchased Countrywide, the largest mortgage lender in this country, and Merrill Lynch, the largest stock brokerage firm in the country. That is how Bank of America expanded. They were too big to fail. Today they are much bigger.

In 2008, JPMorgan Chase, which received a $25 billion bailout from the Bush Treasury Department and a $29 billion bridge loan from the Federal Reserve, acquired Bear Stearns and Washington Mutual, the largest savings and loan in the country. That is how JPMorgan Chase, a huge bank, became even bigger.

In 2008, the Treasury Department provided an $18 billion tax break to Wells Fargo to purchase Wachovia, allowing that bank to control 11 percent of all bank deposits in this country.

Hear this because this is quite unbelievable: When we try to understand what is going on in the economy today—the rich getting richer, the poor getting poorer, the middle class collapsing—today, after we bailed out all these large banks, three out of four of them are now much larger than they were before. Today, Bank of America, JPMorgan Chase, Citigroup, and Wells Fargo—the four largest financial institutions in this country—hold about $7.4 trillion in assets, and that is equal to over half the nation's estimated total output last year. Four financial institutions have assets worth more than 52 percent of our total output last year.

Instead of breaking up these folks, these large institutions, we let them get bigger. In fact, according to Simon Johnson, the former chief economist of the International Monetary Fund:

"As a result of the crisis and various government rescue efforts, the largest six banks in our economy now have total assets in excess [he claims] of 63 percent of GDP. . . . This is a significant increase from even 2006, when the same banks' assets were around 55 percent of GDP. . . ."

Do you understand what this is about? Four financial institutions owning over half the assets of America. You talk about economic power, you talk about political power, that is what we are talking about.

Simon Johnson continues: This is "a complete transformation compared with the situation in the U.S. just 15 years ago—when the six largest banks had combined assets of only around 17 percent of GDP."

So 15 years ago, 17 percent, six banks; today, six banks, and, he claims, 63 percent of GDP. In other words, over the last 15 years, the largest banks in this country have more than tripled in size.

Not only are too-big-to-fail financial institutions bad for taxpayers, the enormous concentration of ownership in the financial sector has led to higher bank fees, usurious interest rates on credit cards, and fewer choices for consumers. What do you think happens when you have a few institutions, a handful of institutions, controlling mortgage lending or where people get their credit cards?

Today, these huge financial institutions have become so big that according to the *Washington Post*: "The four largest banks in America now issue one out of every two mortgages, two out of three credit cards, and hold about $4 out of every $10 in bank deposits in the entire country."

If any of these financial institutions were to get into major trouble again, taxpayers would be on the hook for another substantial bailout. We cannot allow that to happen. So the whole reason for the bailout was that if any of these financial institutions collapsed, it would take down a significant part of the economy and millions of jobs. We had to prop them up. We had to bail them out. It turns out that since we bailed them out, these handful of financial institutions are now even larger than they were before and we now know they are enjoying very strong profits and they are paying their CEOs even more in compensation than they did before the breakdown.

In my view, if we are serious about understanding why the middle class is collapsing, if we are serious about getting this economy moving again long term, we have to have the courage to do exactly what Teddy Roosevelt did back in the trust-busting days and break up these banks. The point Roosevelt was making was, it is bad for the economy when a handful of entities control industry after industry. They have a stranglehold on the economy. You have to break them up. Yet I have heard very little discussion—I know there was an amendment from *Sherrod Brown* and *Ted Kaufman*, and I introduced legislation on this issue to start breaking them up. But, frankly, their lobbyists and their money are such that it becomes very difficult to do that. But that is exactly what we should be doing.

The legislation I introduced last year, S. 2746, the Too Big to Fail, Too Big to Exist Act, would break up these large financial institutions. That legislation would require the Secretary of Treasury to identify every single financial institution and insurance company in this country that is too big to fail within 90 days; and after one year, the Secretary of the Treasury would be required to break up these institutions so their failure would not lead to the collapse of the U.S. or global economies.

I think that is pretty obvious. We passed a financial reform bill, which I supported and got a major provision in there asking for disclosure at the Fed, an investigation of conflicts of interest at the Fed, and an audit of the Fed during the financial crisis. But overall, I by no means think that legislation went anywhere near far enough. I think that is a modest piece of legislation and an issue we have to revisit.

I worry very much about the future because I have a feeling in my stomach that day is going to come around again, when these huge financial institutions are tottering, when they are going to go running to Washington, and they are going to say: Hey, you have to bail us out. In my view, if an institution is too big to fail, it is too big to exist. Let us break them up so we do not have to go through another bailout of Wall Street.

Furthermore, I believe when you have that kind of concentration of ownership—when you have four large financial institutions holding half the mortgages in this country, controlling two-thirds of the credit cards, and amassing 40 percent of all deposits—this is not good for a competitive economy.

We are supposed to be living in free market capitalism, real competition. This is not free market competition. This is a huge concentration of ownership, where a few people have enormous power over the economy, and with their wealth, the political life of this country.

No single financial institution should be so large that its failure would cause catastrophic risk to millions of American jobs or to our nation's economic well-being. No single financial institution should have holdings so extensive that its failure could send the world's economy into crisis. We were there two years ago, and in many ways, despite the passage of the financial reform bill, we are even more there now. The big, huge financial institutions we bailed out are bigger, more huge today.

Interestingly enough, on that issue, it is not just progressives such as myself who hold that view. There are some pretty conservative folks who are honest conservatives. The concentration of ownership in a handful of entities: is that a conservative proposition? Not in terms of my understanding of what conservatives are about. I do not think so.

You have at least three Federal Reserve Bank presidents who support breaking up too-big-to-fail banks. James Bullard, president and chief executive of the Federal Reserve Bank of Saint Louis; Kansas City Fed President Thomas M. Hoenig; and Dallas Fed President Richard W. Fisher—these guys do not have my political views. I am a proud progressive. My guess is they are conservatives. But anybody with an ounce of brains in their head understands that four large financial institutions that have assets that are more than half the GDP of the United States of America places us, A, in a very dangerous position in terms of too big to fail, and, B, it is just bad for a competitive economy.

Is there any wonder why people are paying 25 percent or 30 percent interest rates on their credit cards? That is because these guys issue two-thirds of the credit cards in America. Is there any reason why they were issuing fraudulent mortgage packages to people? Because there is not the kind of competition that should be there.

But this is not just Bernie Sanders' point of view. Here is what Kansas City Fed President Hoenig said in March 2010. This is Kansas City Fed President Hoenig: "I think they should be broken up. I think there's no reason why as we've done in other instances of [sic] finding the right mechanism to break them into their components. . . ."

"And in doing so, I think you'll make the financial system itself more stable. I think you will make it more competitive, and I think you will have long-run benefits over our current system, [which] mixes it and therefore leads to bailouts when crises occur."

This is Thomas Hoenig, the head of the Kansas City Fed. A very simple statement. He is absolutely right. But—and I am going to get to the reason why in a little while—we have not been able to do this. We have not been able to do this because Wall Street sends their lobbyists down here in droves and Wall Street provides zillions of dollars in campaign contributions and Wall Street fights like the dickens to make sure that any strong provisions that some of us might bring up are defeated. Here is what the President of the Dallas Fed, Mr. Fisher, said: "[B]ased on my experience at the Fed . . . the marginal costs of too-big-to-fail financial institutions easily dwarf their purported social and macroeconomic benefits."

"The risk posed by coddling too-big-to-fail banks is simply too great."

Winston Churchill said that. He is quoting Mr. Churchill: "In finance, everything that is agreeable is unsound and everything that is sound is disagreeable."

That is from Churchill.

Mr. Fisher continues: "I think the disagreeable but sound thing to do regarding institutions that are too big to fail is to dismantle them over time into institutions that can be prudently managed and regulated across borders. This should be done before the next financial crisis because we now know it surely cannot be done in the middle of a crisis."

That is Dallas Fed President Mr. Fisher.

They are already in the process of breaking up big banks in England. According to the *Washington Post* on November 3, 2009.

"The British government announced Tuesday—"

Not this Tuesday, November 3, 2009—

"that it will break up parts of major financial institutions bailed out by taxpayers. The British government, spurred on by European regulators, is forcing the Royal Bank of Scotland, Lloyds Banking Group, and Northern Rock to sell off parts of their operations. Europeans are calling for more and smaller banks to increase competition and to eliminate banks so large that they must be rescued by taxpayers, no matter how they conducted their business, in order to avoid damaging the global financial system."

A very interesting development occurred on October 15 of last year. On October 15—as I mentioned earlier, Alan Greenspan, who was the chairman of the Fed before Mr. Bernanke, and I have had our run-ins. Mr. Greenspan, along with Mr. Rubin and others, were the chief proponents—Larry Summers too—were the chief proponents of deregulation of financial institutions, and Mr. Greenspan and I had more than a few arguments. But on October 15 of last year, Alan Greenspan, admitted his views on deregulation were wrong—and I give the man courage for at least admitting he was wrong. He did a heck of a lot of damage, but at least he had the courage to admit he was wrong. He was quoted in Bloomberg News as saying:

"If they are too big to fail, they are too big. In 1911, we broke up Standard Oil. So what happened? The individual parts became more valuable than the whole."

Maybe that's what we need to do.

Alan Greenspan, the architect of deregulation, citing the fact that in 1911 we broke up Standard Oil. So here we have Greenspan, who helped cause this crisis, at least having the courage to understand that now is the time to begin breaking up these big financial institutions. They have enormous power over our economy. They have enormous power over our political life. Their lobbyists are all over this place. You can't walk down the hall without bumping into some of their lobbyists. So we have to start breaking them up and the American people have to be prepared for a major fight to take on these huge financial institutions.

Former Fed Chairman Paul Volcker, who has advised the Obama administration, supports breaking up big banks so they no longer pose systemic risk to the entire economy.

According to an October 20, 2009, article in the *New York Times*, Volcker said: "People say I'm old-fashioned and banks can no longer be separated from nonbank activity. That argument brought us to where we are today."

Paul Volcker. I couldn't agree more. That is what I am talking about. We have to start breaking up four financial institutions which led us into the economic disaster we are in right now that remain much too big to fail, that we are going to have to bail out again and again and again, and that today have a stranglehold on our economy.

The *New York Times* says under Volcker's plan: "JPMorgan Chase would have to give up their trading operations acquired from Bear Stearns. Bank of America and Merrill Lynch would go back to being separate companies. Goldman Sachs could no longer be a bank holding company."

That is exactly what needs to be happening.

I come from a small state. We have community banks. Here is the irony: The banks in Vermont, in the midst of all of this financial disaster, did just fine. They are small, locally owned banks. They know the people they lend money to. The CEOs are not making hundreds of millions of dollars in profit. They know their community. They know what loans make sense. Now, I may be old-fashioned like Mr. Volcker, but I think that is what banking is about: to lend out money to people in the productive economy, to the business community, who can use the money to expand and create jobs; to homeowners who need that money to buy a home—not to be living in your own world engaged in a huge gambling casino producing and selling worthless products nobody understands.

The function of a bank is to be a middleman between people who need money and are producing real products and helping them get that money and people who are investing in the banks. It is not supposed to be an island to itself. But in recent years what we have seen, incredibly, is that about 40 percent of all profit in America went to the financial institutions with a small number of people working there, relatively small. They got about 40 percent of the profits because they live in a world that is a huge gambling casino.

We need financial institutions to go back to the way banking used to be, where the job of banks was to provide affordable loans to the productive economy so we can produce real products, real goods, and we can create real jobs when we do that.

Robert Reich, President Clinton's former labor secretary, said: "No important public interest is served by allowing giant banks to grow too big to fail. Wall Street banks should be split up, and soon."

We have a lot of people, some conservatives, some progressives, who are saying the same thing. If we are going to rebuild the middle class, the way to do that is, among other things, to change our disastrous trade policies, to make it clear to corporate America that they cannot continue to sell out the workers of this country by moving to China and other low-wage countries. We also have to have a much more competitive economy, one in which all large financial institutions do not own assets of more than half of the GDP of this country.

On that point, I find it very interesting that it is not just progressives such as myself or Robert Reich, but we have some conservative bankers—people who are heading Fed banks around this country—who are saying pretty much the same thing.

Also, when we talk about banks, I wish to get back to a point I raised earlier. This is an issue I have been working on for years and years, and this is the issue of usury. I mentioned earlier, if you read the religious tenents of the major religions throughout history, whether it is Christianity, Judaism, Islam, and others, what you find is almost universal objection and disgust and a feeling of immorality in terms of usury. When we talked about usury in the United States, what we usually talked about were thugs, gangsters working on street corners who lent out money at outrageously high interest rates to workers, and when that money was not repaid at the interest rates asked for, the thugs would beat up the workers.

In fact, I am thinking now about the first movie of *Rocky*. I don't know if the Presiding Officer saw the first movie of *Rocky* with Sylvester Stallone, but before he became a successful fighter and the heavyweight champion of the world, that is what he was: a big tough guy who beat up people who did not pay back the gangsters the high interest rates they were asking for.

Well, the world has changed. Now the people who are committing usury are not the gangsters on street corners all over America. Their place has been taken by the CEOs of Wall Street financial institutions who are lending out money to desperate Americans at 25 or 30 percent interest rates. That, my friends, is called usury, and according to every religion on Earth, that is immoral. What you are doing is going up to people who are desperate, people who are hurting, and you are saying: You desperately need money, we are going to give you money, but there is a string attached. You are going to be charged an outrageous amount of interest on that money.

So here is the irony: The people who are hurting the most pay the highest interest rates. The people who need the money the least are paying the lowest interest rates.

So the Fed lent out billions and billions of dollars to the largest financial institutions and offered it at less than 1 percent. That is American taxpayer money—large corporations, less than 1 percent.

But if you are a worker today and you are having hard times—maybe you are unemployed—you are going to pay 25 or 30 percent interest rates on your credit card, and sometimes more. You have this Payday Lending where people are paying outrageous sums of money. I think that is immoral. I think we have to stop it, and it disturbs me very much that especially at a time when we bailed out these large financial institutions they are still able to charge our people 25 or 30 percent. People who have bailed them out get hit the second time around by having to pay 25 to 30 percent interest rates.

Right now, it is not even 25 or 30 percent. As a matter of fact, the tenth largest credit card issuer in this country, an entity called Premier Bank, is now offering a credit card with a 79.9 percent interest rate and a $300 credit limit. What do we make of that? The tenth largest credit card issuer in this country is charging 79 percent interest rates, and we allow that to go on. These are crooks. These are no different than the gangsters who beat up people on street corners when they didn't get payment back, except now the gangsters are wearing three-piece suits and sitting in some fancy suite on Wall Street.

Today, over one-quarter of all credit card holders in this country are now paying interest rates above 20 percent and, as I indicated, as high as 79 percent. Let's be clear. When credit card companies charge over 20 percent interest on credit cards, they are not engaged in the business of making credit available. What they are involved in is extortion and loan sharking—nothing essentially different than gangsters, except they dress a lot better. That is all it is. It is thievery and we tolerate it, and we bail them out.

It is interesting in terms of these high interest rates because for many years we have had states, including the State of Vermont, saying: You are not going to charge outrageously high interest rates. For example, establishing a usury law is not a radical concept, which is what we have to move toward. We have to put a cap on interest rates. In fact, over 20 states in America have laws capping interest rates.

In Alabama, the legal maximum amount of interest is 8 percent; in Alaska, it is 10.5 percent; in Arizona, it is 10 percent; in Idaho, 12 percent; Kansas, 15 percent; the State of Vermont, my own state, the legal maximum interest rate is 12 percent. But what happened is all of those state interest rate caps disappeared under the 1978 U.S. Supreme Court decision known as the Marquette case, which allowed banks to charge whatever interest rates they wanted if they moved to a state without an interest rate law such as South Dakota or Delaware.

So all of these companies moved to South Dakota. They moved to Delaware. No interest rates limits. And they charged the people in Vermont or Hawaii or anyplace else 35 percent interest rates.

So getting back to the original agreement—which I strongly disagree with—that the President and the Republican leadership agreed to, I think that agreement significantly helps the upper income people by lowering the tax rates for millionaires and billionaires, by lowering the estate tax, and by providing some business tax breaks which are not the kinds of investments that can best create jobs.

(The PRESIDENT pro tempore assumed the chair.)

One of the things we have to do to protect the middle class today is have a cap on interest rates because otherwise people are getting a paycheck and then going into debt and paying 25, 30 percent interest rates, with the money going to a handful of banks on Wall Street.

I have introduced legislation to put a cap on interest rates, and it is not a radical idea. Right now, credit unions in this country, by law, are not allowed to charge more than 15 percent, except under extraordinary circumstances. By and large, that has worked for about 30 years. So if you get a credit card through a credit union, you are going to be paying in almost every case no more than 15 percent. That was developed by Federal law.

Do you know what? I have talked to the credit union people in Vermont and all over the country. Credit unions are doing just fine. They are not the ones that came begging the American taxpayer for a huge bailout. So for 30 years they have survived just fine on a 15 percent cap. But our friends on Wall Street who caused this recession, our friends on Wall Street who needed a welfare check from the American people in order to survive, who today are earning more money than they did before the bailout—we don't have any cap on the interest rates they can charge.

In my view, if the credit unions have survived and survived well with a 15 percent maximum interest rate cap—the most they can charge—and it worked for credit unions, it can work for the private banks as well. That is what we have to do.

According to a March 15, 2009, article—this is a year ago—in the *Los Angeles Times*: "Chris Collver, legislative and regulatory analyst for the California Credit Union League, said that a rate cap hasn't hurt business for nearly 400 credit unions represented by his organization. 'It hasn't been an issue,' he said. 'Credit unions are still able to thrive.'"

Here is my point. The middle class is hurting. Unemployment is outrageously high, poverty is increasing, there are 50 million people with no health insurance, there is a gap between the rich and everybody else, manufacturing is collapsing, and jobs are going all over the world—China, Mexico, India. We have to start protecting the middle class of this country.

There are a number of things we have to do. I think one simple thing we have to do is tell the crooks on Wall Street—and I use that word advisedly—history will prove that they knew what they were doing. They were dishonest. The business model is fraudulent. There are honest people who occasionally make a mistake, but there are other businesses that are based on fraud and assume they are never going to get caught. When they do get caught, the penalty they have to pay is so little that it is worth it because they end up getting caught 1 out of 10 times, but they make a whole lot of money, and then they pay a fine and somebody goes to jail—very rarely, though—for a year. That is what you are seeing on Wall Street.

I think if it has worked very well for the credit unions, it can work for the private banks as well.

Mr. President, in the financial reform bill, did we address this issue? Yes, we did, and no, we didn't. We said the credit card companies have to be clearer and more honest about their interest rates and how much borrowing money will actually cost because before they would say: You will get a zero interest rate or a 2 percent interest rate, but most people didn't read the small print on page 4 that said they could raise interest rates at any time.

We have made some progress on at least them being honest with the American people about what their credit card costs will be, but that is not enough. What we have to do is put a cap on interest rates. It has worked for the credit unions. I believe it can and should work for the big banks as well.

Mr. President, what I want to do now is just give you some examples about—you know, sometimes here—and I am guilty of it as well—we talk in big numbers—a billion here and a trillion there—and it adds up. But I think it is also important to look at the flesh and blood that is out there, the real suffering people are experiencing.

A while back, what I did was I sent an e-mail out to people in Vermont. It was a very simple e-mail. It said: Tell me in your own words what is going on in your family. What is going on in your lives, in the midst of this terrible recession?

Again, it is important. Yes, we know unemployment is 9.8 percent and the real unemployment is 17 percent, 50 million people don't have any health insurance, median family income has gone down, poverty has gone up, and 25 percent of our kids are on food stamps. It is important to know that stuff. But behind all of those statistics is flesh and blood and good people who are doing everything they can to survive with a shred of dignity in their lives.

I did this two years ago. I sent that e-mail out to my constituents in Vermont, and I said: Write back to me. Tell me in your own words what is going on in your lives. I cannot remember how many we received, but there were hundreds and hundreds of responses. It quite amazed me. Frankly, it was hard to read these letters from decent, good people about what was happening in their lives.

What I said to them was this: If it is OK with you, we will publish what you have written. We won't use your names, of course. I don't want to embarrass anybody. We will read some of these stories on the floor of the Senate.

That is what I did. I didn't read them all, but I read some of them because it is important for us sitting here inside the

Beltway not to forget what is going on in the real world, whether it is Hawaii, Vermont, California, or anyplace.

Here are letters from two mothers in Vermont. The first is from a woman in a rural area. The second is from a single mother in a small city. In Vermont, frankly, we don't have too many big cities. In my very beautiful state, where I expect the weather is very cold today, our largest city is all of 40,000 people. That is Burlington, Vermont, and I was honored to have been the mayor of that city for eight years. Certainly, the vast majority of our people live in towns of less than 1,000, and there are towns of 500. For a while, I lived in a town called Stannard, up in the Northeast Kingdom of Vermont, which has probably 150 people in it, and that is not uncommon in Vermont. There are a lot of small towns.

Here are the two letters.

A woman in the rural area says: "My husband and I have lived in Vermont our whole lives. We have two small children, a baby and a toddler, and have felt fortunate to own our own house and land. But due to the increasing fuel prices, we have at times had to choose between baby food and diapers and heating fuel."

In Vermont, heating fuel gets up there when the weather gets 20 below zero. It is an expensive proposition.

Continuing:

"We have run out of heating fuel three times so far, and the baby has ended up in the hospital with pneumonia two of the times. We tried to keep the kids warm with an electric space heater on those nights, but that just doesn't do the trick. My husband does what he can just to scrape enough money for car fuel each week, and we have gone from three vehicles to one just to try to get by without going further into debt. We were going to sell the house and rent, but the rent around here is higher than what we pay for our mortgage and property taxes combined. Please help."

That is what she asked of me and her government—"Please help." She didn't ask me to lower taxes for billionaires. She is speaking for tens of millions of people in this country who are in desperate need of help.

Here is another letter that came from a woman who lives in a larger town: "I am a single mother with a 9-year-old boy. We lived this past winter without any heat at all."

That is not a good position to be in in Vermont in the winter.

"Fortunately, someone gave me an old wood stove. I had to hook it up to an old unused chimney we had in the kitchen. I couldn't even afford a chimney liner. The price of liners went up with the price of fuel. To stay warm at night, my son and I would pull off all the pillows from the couch and pile them on the kitchen floor. I would hang a blanket from the kitchen doorway, and we would sleep right there on the floor. By February, we ran out of wood, and I burned my mother's dining room furniture. I have no oil for hot water. We boil our water on the stove and pour it into the tub. I would like to order one of your flags and hang it upside down at the Capitol building. We are certainly a country in distress."

Mr. President, what I will without doubt assure you is that those stories, in different forms—and I know it is different in big cities than in a rural state such as Vermont, and I know it is different in Hawaii, where the Chair comes from, than in Boston, Massachusetts. But I am absolutely sure that millions of people in one way or another are telling the same story. These are great Americans, people who want to work and do the best they can by their kids. They are simply not making it right now.

This is the United States of America, in 2010, and people are going cold. People don't have enough food. People are homeless. My friends here are talking about huge tax breaks for billionaires. My friends here are talking about lowering rates on the estate tax for the top three-tenths of 1 percent of the American people. What are we talking about? What kinds of priorities are those?

Here is another letter from Vermont. This is not a woman in desperation. Those folks I just read from are. This woman says:

"As a couple with one child, earning about $55,000 a year [which is, in Vermont, fairly decent] we have been able to eat out a bit, buy groceries and health insurance, contribute to our retirement funds, and live a relatively comfortable life financially. We have never accumulated a lot of savings, but our bills were always paid on time, and we never had any interest on our credit card. Over the last year, even though we have tightened our belts, not eating out much, watching purchases at the grocery store, not buying extras like a new

TV, and repairing the washer instead of buying a new one—
doing all those things, we find ourselves with over $7,000 of
credit card debt and are trying to figure out how to pay for
braces for our son. I work 50 hours per week to help earn extra money to catch up. But that also takes a toll on the family
life. Not spending those 10 hours at home with my husband
and son makes a big difference for all of us. My husband
hasn't had a raise in three years and his employer is looking
to cut out any extra benefits they can to lower their ex-
penses, which will increase ours."

How many millions of Americans do you think are saying
exactly the same thing?

Let me read another story that comes from Vermont:

"My 90-year-old father in Connecticut has recently become ill and asked me to visit him. I want to drop everything
I am doing and go visit him. However, I am finding it hard to
save enough money to add to the extra gas I will need to get
there. I am self-employed with my own commercial cleaning
service and money is tight, not only with gas prices but with
everything. I make more than I did a year ago, and I don't
have enough to pay my property taxes this quarter for the
first time in many years. They are due tomorrow."

Here is another letter that I think deserves to be read. Mr.
President, I think it would not hurt this body if every Member of the Senate—I know we all get letters like this—came
down here and spent a couple of days talking about what is
going on with working families in this country. Spouting statistics is good, and dealing with tax deals of $900 billion is

fine, but I think we should reacquaint ourselves with the reality of life in America today.

This is what another constituent of mine writes:

"My husband and I are retired and 65 years of age. We
would have liked to work longer, but because of injuries
caused at work and the closing of our factory to go to Can-
ada, we chose to retire early. Now, with oil prices the way
they are, we cannot afford to heat our home unless my husband cuts and splits wood, which is a real hardship as he has
had his back fused and should not be working most of the
day to keep up with the wood. Not only that, he has to get up
two or three times each night to keep the fire going."

In other words, what she is talking about, is that in Vermont a lot of people heat with wood—increasingly with pel-
lets, an important source of fuel in the State of Vermont.
What she is talking about is her husband, who is 65, with a
bad back, has to go out and cut wood, and in their case, his
being old, he has to get up two or three times a night to
stoke the furnace that is keeping the house warm. Again, I
would remind people that in Vermont it occasionally gets 20
or 30 below zero.

She continues: "We also have a 2003 car that we only get
to drive to get groceries or go to the doctor or to visit my
mother in the nursing home three miles away. It now costs
us $80 a month to go nowhere. We have 42,000 miles on a
five-year-old car."

They can't afford to even use the car. I don't know what
the price of gas is in Hawaii, Mr. President, but in Vermont it

is now over $3 a gallon. A lot of people in my state have to travel long distances to get to work. Their cars need repairs. Cars break down. Cars require, in Vermont, compulsory insurance. They have to spend a whole lot of money just getting to work. I think we forget about that here. We don't need tax breaks for billionaires, we need to pay attention to these people.

She continues and concludes: "I have Medicare, but I can't afford prescription coverage unless I take my money out of an annuity, which is supposed to cover the house payment when my husband's pension is gone. We only eat two meals a day to conserve."

This is not some Third World country. This is the United States of America, my state of Vermont, and Vermont is better off today than a number of states around this country. You have these stories, and multiply them by 10 in every area of this country.

Here is another story:

"Yesterday, I paid for our latest home heating fuel delivery—"

Again, I am focusing now on the cost of fuel because in Vermont, where I come from, it is a big deal. So she writes:

"Yesterday, I paid for our latest home fuel heating delivery—$1,100. I also paid my $2,000-plus credit card balance, much of which bought gas and groceries for the month."

The point here, and then I will continue her letter, is that a lot of people use their credit cards not just as a nice and convenient way of not having to use cash—when I go shopping, I am going to use my credit card and I will pay it off at the end of the month. What a nice thing. No, people are using their credit cards to buy food, to buy gas, and to buy the basic necessities of life. It is their only line of credit open. And then, as I mentioned earlier, they are charged 25 or 30 percent interest rates on what they owe.

She continues:

"My husband and I are very nervous about what will happen to us when we are old. Although we have three jobs between us and participate in 403(b) retirement plans, we have not saved enough for a realistic post–work-life if we survive to our life expectancy. As we approach the traditional retirement age, we are slowly paying off our daughter's college tuition loan and trying to keep our heads above water. We have always lived frugally. We buy used cars and store brand groceries, recycle everything, walk or car pool, when possible, and plastic our windows each fall."

What that means is that, in Vermont, if you don't have good storm windows, you put up plastic. It is a way to keep the wind out and keep the home warm. I know about that because I used to do that.

"Even so, if and when our son decides to attend college, we will be in deep debt at age 65. Please—"

And here she ends this. "P.S. Please don't use my name. I live in a small town, and this is so embarrassing."

So embarrassing. We should be embarrassed, not her. We should be embarrassed that we are for one second talking about a proposal which gives tax breaks to billionaires while we are ignoring the needs of working families, low-income people, and the middle class. We should be embarrassed that we are not investing in our infrastructure, that we are not breaking up these large financial institutions, that we are not putting a cap on interest rates, that we are the only country in the world that does not have health care for all of our people—of major countries. We should be embarrassed, not this wonderful woman who is trying to maintain her dignity.

Another letter from the State of Vermont:

"I too have been struggling to overcome the increasing cost of gas, heating oil, food, taxes, et cetera. I have to say that this is the toughest year financially that I have ever experienced in my 41 years on this Earth. I have what used to be considered a decent job. I work hard, pinch my pennies, but the pennies have all but dried up. I am thankful that my employer understands that many of us cannot afford to drive to work five days a week. Instead, I work three 15-hour days. I have taken odd jobs to try to make ends meet. This winter, after keeping the heat just high enough to keep my pipes from bursting—"

One of the problems you have, when you live in a rural state and it gets cold, your pipes can burst, and then you have to spend a fortune getting them repaired.

She continues: "The bedrooms are not heated and never go above 30 degrees."

What happens in Vermont, if you have a home, in the wintertime, and you don't have a whole lot of money, you kind of close off rooms in the house because you can't afford to heat the whole house. So people live in a smaller area.

She continues: "I began selling off my woodworking tools, snow blower, pennies on the dollar, and furniture that had been handed down in my family from the early 1800s just to keep the heat on. Today, I am sad, broken and very discouraged. I am thankful the winter cold is behind us for a while but now gas prices are rising yet again. I just can't keep up."

That is the story from one person in Vermont. But that is the story for millions and millions of Americans.

Another story. And the reason I am reading these stories—and I appreciate my staff bringing this booklet down here—is this puts flesh and blood and real life into the statistics. The statistics are frightening enough, but this tells us what happens when the middle class of this country collapses. It tells us what happens when people lose decent-paying jobs. It tells us what happens when the government does not provide the kind of basic support system that it should for people in need.

Here is another letter: "As a single parent, I am struggling every day to put food on the table."

Mr. President, this is the United States of America and people are talking, in my State of Vermont and all over the country, about struggling to put food on the table. What comes to my mind now—and I don't know if you saw them, Mr. President—are some articles in the paper that talked about because of the bailing out of Wall Street, and the fact that Wall Street is now again profitable, these executives there are now making more money than they made before the bailout, and they go into restaurants and they pay thousands of dollars for a bottle of wine, pay hundreds and hundreds of dollars for some fancy dinner. Yet in my state and all over this country there are people who are wondering where their next meal is coming from.

She continues: "Our clothing all comes from thrift stores. I have a five-year-old car that needs work. My son is gifted and talented. I tried to sell my house to enroll him in a school that had curriculum available for his special needs. After two years on the market, my house never sold. The property taxes have nearly doubled in 10 years."

Let me pick up on that point. We don't deal with property taxes here—I did when I was a mayor—but if we are not adequately funding education, if we do not adequately help cities and towns all over this country in terms of fire protection and in terms of police protection and housing, a lot of that burden falls on the very regressive property tax, which in my State of Vermont is very high. And you find it referred to time and time again that property taxes are going up. Property taxes are going up.

She writes: "Property taxes have nearly doubled in 10 years. And the oil to heat is prohibitive. To meet the needs of my son, I have left the house sit and moved into an apartment near his high school. I don't go to church many Sundays because the gasoline is too expensive to drive there."

Imagine: She doesn't go to church on Sundays because the gasoline is too expensive to drive there.

"Every thought of an activity is dependent upon the cost. I can only purchase food from dented can stores."

Does anybody in this Congress know what a dented can store is? Do you know that many people buy their groceries and they get them cheaper because the cans are dented? Most Members of the Senate and the House, most Governors do not get their meals from dented cans, but huge numbers of Americans do.

She then concludes: "I am stretched to the breaking point with no help in sight."

By the way, the letters that I received, when I asked for letters, came not just from the State of Vermont—most came from Vermont but some came from other areas. I will read another from Vermont and then one from rural Pennsylvania.

This one from Vermont: "Due to illness, my ability to work has been severely limited. I am making $10 an hour, and if I am lucky, I get 35 hours a week of work."

Let me pull away from the letter. That is not an unusual wage in the State of Vermont. That is not an unusual wage all over America. That is what people earn, $10 an hour, times 40 hours. He doesn't get 40 hours. He makes $350 a week. Ten times 40, 400, times 50, $21,000 a year. Shock of all shocks, that is reality. That is what people are trying to live on. Those are the people that we should be helping, not the CEOs on Wall Street who will get $1 million a year in a tax break if this deal goes through. Not the people who are in the top three-tenths of 1 percent, who our Republican friends want to help by repealing the estate tax, which will cost us about $1 trillion in 10 years. Maybe we should concentrate on helping people who are trying to get by eating food from dented cans or people who can't afford to drive to church on Sunday because they can't afford the price of a gallon of gas. Maybe we should remember who sent us here and who made this country.

He writes: "I am making $10 an hour, and if I am lucky I get 35 hours a week of work. At this time, I am only getting 20 hours, as it is off season in Stowe."

Stowe, Vermont, is a beautiful town. I hope everybody comes to visit us up there. There is great skiing, but it is a resort town. Big time in the winter. We are doing better in the summer, but it is a resort town. Resorts get more business in the winter than summer and less time elsewhere.

So what he is talking about is that it is off season up there and he is only getting 20 hours a week of work at $10 an hour.

He writes: "It does not take a mathematician to do the figures."

"How are my wife and I supposed to live on a monthly take-home income of less than $800 a month? We do it by spending our hard-earned retirement savings. I am 50 and my wife is 49. At the rate we are going, we will be destitute in just a few years. The situation is so dire it is all that I can think about. Soon I will have to start walking to work—an eight-mile round trip—because the price of energy is so high that it is either that or going without heat."

This is a 50-year-old guy, making $10 an hour, 20 or 30 hours a week, and his choice is either walking 8 miles to and from his job in Stowe or else not heating his home. And this happens in Vermont all of the time. It is quite unbelievable.

He says: "As bad as our situation is, I know many in worse shape. We try to donate food when we do our weekly shopping, but now we are not able to even afford to help our neighbors eat. What has this country come to?"

I don't know about other parts of the country. I am sure it is the same. But if you go to a grocery store, there is often a bin out there in front where people buy food and they drop a can of peas or a can of corn or something into it. Here is a guy who is now faced with the reality of having to walk eight miles to and from work and he is upset at himself that he does not have the money to buy food for his neighbors who he thinks are even worse off than he is. That is the good people of Vermont and America. They are all over this country, good and decent people who do worry about their neighbors.

Then you have the lobbyists here representing the largest corporations in the world where the CEOs make tens of millions of dollars a year and their job is to squeeze the middle class and these families harder and harder, cut back on their benefits in order to give tax breaks to the richest people in this country. What a difference in attitude: A poor man faced with the choice of either walking eight miles to and from his job or losing his heat, worried about his neighbors, and you have the lobbyists here worrying about the richest people in the world—and winning. And winning.

Then I got a letter that comes not from Vermont, it comes from rural Pennsylvania:

"I am 55 years old and worse off than my adult children. I have worked since age 16. I don't live from paycheck to paycheck, I live day to day. I can only afford to fill my gas tank on my payday. Thereafter I put $5, $10, whatever that I can. I cannot afford to buy the food items that I would. I am riding around daily, to and from work, with a quarter of a tank of gas. This is very scary. I can see myself working until the day that I die."

Trust me, the gentleman is talking about getting older, worrying about working until the day he dies. We are already seeing this. You go to grocery stores in Vermont and you see old people, who should be sitting home with their grandchildren. Do you know what they are doing? They are packing groceries. Then we have some geniuses on this deficit reduction commission, people who made their money on Wall Street, they have a brilliant idea: Let's raise the Social Security age to 68, 69 years old so that people like this will have to work, in fact, to the day they die.

He continues. This is not from Vermont. This is from Pennsylvania:

"I do not have savings, no credit cards and my only resources are through my employment. I have to drive to work as there are no buses from my residence to work. I don't know how much longer I can do this. I am concerned as gas prices climb daily. I am just tired. The harder that I work the harder it gets. I work 12 to 14 hours daily and it just doesn't help."

I am not saying every person in America is experiencing these stories. They are not. A lot of people are doing fine.

They have good jobs. Their kids are doing well. They are taking care of their parents. A lot of people are doing just fine. But we would be fools and dishonest not to understand the reality of what is going on in this country. It breaks my heart, and I know it breaks the hearts of millions of people in this country, to see what is going on in this great Nation of ours: that so many people are hurting, that so many parents—I don't know if I have that letter or if it is in another booklet. I will never forget one letter I received, and that is these people—my parents never went to college. My father never graduated high school. They wanted their kids to get an education; that is what they wanted—and we did. It was very important, and how proud my mother was of that.

We get letters from people who say: You know, I dreamed that my kid, my daughter, would go to college, and she is not going to go to college now. She is not going to go to college.

It is just painful to even talk about and think about the direction in which this country is moving. So I want to now take a break from reading these letters. Actually, the truth is, when these letters came in a year ago I could not read more than a half dozen at a time. They took too much out of me. They take something out of you to hear people you know, good people, honest people—I hear from some of my colleagues here that people are lazy. My God, people work so hard in the State of Vermont. We have I don't know how many thousands of people are not working just two or three jobs, they work four jobs. It is all over this country. Whatever you say about the United States of America, the people of our country are not lazy. That is one thing you can say about them.

In fact, according to all of the bloodless statistics, our people today work longer hours than do the people of any other major country on Earth. Did you know that? I don't know that a lot of Americans know that. It used to be Japan. The Japanese are a very hard-working people. Now it turns out that our people work harder, longer hours than do the people of any other country in the industrialized world.

When you think about that, when I think about the books that I read when I was in elementary school—I remember there were pictures up there. I don't know if you remember these pictures. There were pictures where workers were demonstrating, and they said: We want a 40-hour workweek. Do you remember seeing those pictures? We want a 40-hour workweek. That was back in the early 1900s.

Today, 100 years later, people still want a 40-hour work-week because they are forced to work 50 or 60 hours a week. They are working two jobs. They are working three jobs.

What I want to do now, before I get back to why I am on the Senate floor today, and why I have been here for a few hours—which is to say the agreement negotiated by the President and the Republican leadership is not a good agreement. It is an agreement that we can improve upon. It is an agreement the American people can improve upon. But what I am asking the American people to do is to stand up, let your Senators, let your Congressman know how you feel.

Do you really believe millionaires and billionaires who have done phenomenally well in recent years need an extended tax cut at a time when their taxes have been lowered substantially in recent years? Do we really need to give tax breaks to the rich in order to drive up the national debt so our kids and grandchildren will pay higher taxes in order to pay off that national debt caused by tax breaks for the rich?

If you do not believe that, if you do not think that is right, let the President of the United States know about it. Let your Senator know about it. Let your Congressman know about it. We need a handful, seven or eight Members of the Senate to hear from their people, to say: Wait a minute. Don't hold my kids hostage. Don't force them to pay higher taxes in order to give tax breaks to the very rich.

If the American people stand up and by the millions let their Senators and Congressmen and the President know, we can win this thing. We can win this battle. It is not too late yet. That is what I hope will happen.

When we talk about why things go on the way they are here in Washington, and why so many people back home—whether they are Democrats, Republicans, Independent—whether they are conservatives, progressives, moderates, whatever they are—there is a huge feeling of anger and frustration and, in fact, disgust at what goes on here in Washington.

I have just read some letters from people. You can multiply those letters by one million. People are saying: Don't you hear us? Don't you know what is going on in our lives? Don't you know the worries we have for our kids, for our parents? Aren't you listening to us?

In many ways I am afraid the Senate is not listening to them, nor is the House, nor is our Government. What worries me so much about the growing concentration of wealth and income in this country is that when the rich get richer, they don't just simply put their money under the mattress. They don't simply go out and buy yachts and planes and 18 homes and all the things rich people do. They do that, but they do something else.

They say: I am not rich enough. I need to be richer. What motivates some of these people is greed and greed and more greed. There is no end to it. So what they do is they do things like hire lobbyists—who are all over Capitol Hill. These lobbyists, sometimes former leaders of the Republican Party, former leaders of the Democratic Party, former hotshot lawyers, bright people, their job is to make sure the legislation we pass—such as this major tax bill—that this legislation benefits not ordinary Americans, not the people whose letters I have just read, not those people, but the wealthiest people in this country and the largest corporations.

I want to just mention something. A very good friend of mine and I do a radio show every Friday afternoon—I am afraid I missed it today—Thom Hartmann. Thom is the author of a number of wonderful books.

In his latest book, which is called *Rebooting the American Dream, 11 Ways to Rebuild Our Country*, Thom writes and he talks about lobbying, which is an issue we have to deal with in this country. He says, on page 104: "Given how lucrative lobbying is as an investment, it has become a huge business."

In other words, what he is talking about is, if you have a good lobbyist and the lobbyist changes a few words in a bill, your company or you as an individual can end up with huge amounts of money just by changing a few words. In this case, language that we are working on now is whether we extend the Bush tax breaks for the top 2 percent, for many millionaires and billionaires. Some lobbyists, representing the rich and the powerful, are determined to keep that language in there.

So it is an investment. So you spend a few million dollars, an organization spends a few million dollars on a lobbyist, but if you end up getting back hundreds of millions of dollars in tax breaks and corporate loopholes or other benefits, it is a very good investment. That is what Thom Hartmann is writing. He says: "Given how lucrative lobbying is as an investment it has become a huge business. In February, 2010, the Center for Responsive Politics laid out which industries had invested how much in Congress the previous year. Overall, it found that in 2009 the number of registered lobbyists who actively lobby Congress was 13,694 and the total lobbying spending—"

Get this. Total lobbying spending in 2009 was $3.47 billion, a 240-percent increase since 1999, 10 years, more than tripling it. In 2009 companies spent $3.47 billion in lobbying. We have 100 Members of the Senate, 435 Members of the House. Listeners or viewers can get out their calculating machine and divide it up, how much money the big money interests are spending trying to influence Senator *Inouye* or myself or the other 98 Members of the Senate or 435 Members of the House. They are flooding this institution with money.

Let me give you a breakdown of where that money is coming from. What they call miscellaneous business, that is retail and manufacturing, et cetera, $558 million in one year, 2009; health care, $543 million.

By the way, that was before health care reform. My strong guess—I will be very surprised if that number did not double. If you were a health care lobbyist this year, trust me, you are doing very well. They were all over this place, making sure we did not pass a strong health care bill, for example, a Medicare for all, a single-payer program, which I support.

On top of that, you have the finance, insurance, and real estate industries combined that spent $465 million.

And, again, that was before we dealt with financial reform. I suppose the recent legislation we dealt with, health care reform and financial reform, was a real boon to the lobbyists around here, because they can go out and earn their money. But that was before this. Finance, insurance, real estate, only spent $465 million in one year to influence 100 Members of the Senate and 435 Members of the House.

Energy and natural resources. Well, as I mentioned earlier today, Exxon Mobil last year made $19 billion, paid nothing in federal income taxes, got a $156 million refund according to their SEC filings. Exxon Mobil and other companies are putting all kinds of money into phony organizations telling us that global warming is not real, that we do not have to transform our energy system. It costs a lot of money to do that. The energy and natural resources companies spent $408 million in 2009 alone. This is one year, folks, one year.

Communications, electronics. Right now I am working on an issue which deals with the merger of Comcast and NBC. I think it is a bad idea. Comcast is the largest provider of cable services in America, huge role in the Internet, and NBC is one of the largest media conglomerates in America. What they are trying to do right now is to merge these two huge companies.

I think the problem in America is we have too few companies controlling what goes on. We have too much of a concentration of ownership, and that merger is bad. Well, I can assure you for a fact, they have all of these lobbyists in the media industry, from communications, right here rallying, trying to do their best to make sure this merger and other types of mergers take place—$360 million from the communication and electronics industry.

Then we have other types of organizations as well. Bottom line, in the year 2009, they spent $3.47 billion, almost 3½ billion, on lobbying. And you know what, you get what you pay for.

That is just lobbying. We are not talking about campaign contributions. We are not talking about the huge sums of money it now takes to run for office in the United States, and we are not talking about where that money comes from. We are not talking about the horrendous *Citizens United* decision reached by the Supreme Court which allows billionaires and all of these companies and their executives to put money into campaigns and not even have to be identified. We are not even talking about that. This is just lobbying.

So if you wonder why we are having a serious discussion about whether we should give tax breaks to millionaires and billionaires while the middle class is collapsing, and tens of millions of people have no health insurance, and we have the highest rate of children in poverty, and we have the most unequal distribution of wealth and income of any country, if you wonder how we would consider for one minute talking about more tax breaks for the rich, then you do not know much about what goes on here in Washington and you do not know about campaign contributions and the degree to which big money buys and sells politicians.

I want to review again—the reason I am down here today, and I have been here for a few hours—and voice my very strong opposition to the agreement that was reached between the Republican leadership and President Obama. I think the American people do not like this agreement. All I can tell you—I do not know what is going on in your office, coming from Alaska, Mr. President, but I can tell you in the last three days, between phone calls and e-mails, I probably have gotten 5,000. We have heard from about 5,000 people, many from Vermont, some from out of state as well.

The opposition to this agreement is probably 99 percent. People cannot understand why in a million years, with a $13.8 trillion national debt, and a $1.3 trillion yearly deficit, we would be thinking for one second, for one second, about giving tax breaks to the richest people in this country who are already doing fabulously well.

I am down here today, and have been for a few hours, to urge my colleagues and, more importantly, the American people, to say no to this agreement. If we stand together, if the American people write or e-mail or call their Senators and their Congress people, I think we can turn this thing around. I think we can come up with an agreement that makes us all proud, rather than one that we have to be ashamed of.

I know there was an editorial back in the State of Vermont which I saw. I do not remember the exact title, but something to the effect of: This agreement stinks, it is odious, but it is better than nothing. Well, I do not think that has to be the choice, awful or better than nothing. I think the choice can actually be a good agreement. And I think if the American people stand with those of us who are opposing this agreement, we can pull this off. We can defeat this agreement and come up with a much better one, one that does not cause our kids and grandchildren to pay higher taxes in order to provide huge tax breaks for the richest people in this country.

In talking about the reasons I am opposed to this agreement, one of the other reasons is that while the President and the Republican leadership say, well, you know, this is just a temporary extension, it is going to be for two years, just temporary, you know and I know that when you talk about temporary here, it becomes long term and then perhaps becomes permanent.

If we extend these tax breaks for the top 2 percent now, my strong guess—I hope I am wrong. I certainly hope this proposal is defeated, but if we extend them for two years, my strong guess is they will be, two years from now, extended again. And depending upon the politics of what goes on here, they can be extended permanently.

Our Republican colleagues, as you well know, wanted to extend them for 10 years at a cost of $700 billion. An increase in our national debt. Our Republican friends are fighting hard to completely repeal the estate tax, which would cost us about $1 trillion, $1 trillion in 10 years in increased national debt.

So the point I have got to make—I want to emphasize this point, that when people talk about these things being short term, being temporary, take those thoughts with a grain of salt. Maybe that is the case. I do not think it is. I think once you move over the cliff and make that decision to extend these tax breaks, they are going to be extended long term. Here is the reason why. Right now the dynamic here is the President campaigned against these tax breaks. The President does not believe in extending these tax breaks for the rich. But he felt he had to make the compromise. I thought he made a bad compromise.

But our Republican friends are saying over and over that if you rescind, end these tax breaks to the rich, you are raising taxes two years from now in the midst of a Presidential campaign, when President Obama, if he is the Democratic candidate, says: Do not worry, I am going to oppose these extensions of tax breaks for the rich, his credibility has been severely damaged, and the American people know it. Can they trust him? That is what he told them then. That is what he will tell them in two years. Is he going to be believed? I do not think so. So these tax breaks, while ostensibly for two years may, in fact, be for a lot longer than that.

I would also say that what we have talked about—primarily the discussion has centered around extending the tax breaks, personal income tax breaks to the very rich—there are other tax breaks in this proposal which are equally odious.

What this agreement between the President and the Republican leadership does is it extends the Bush era 15 percent tax rates on capital gains and dividends, meaning that those people who make their living off of their investments will continue to pay a substantially lower tax rate than firemen, teachers, and nurses.

Think about that. You are a big-time investor. You make most of your income off of capital gains or dividends, and you are paying a 15 percent tax rate. But if you are a worker doing something with your hands or you are a teacher or a fireman or you are a cop or nurse, a doctor, you are paying tax rates that are higher than that. We are extending those 15 percent tax rates on capital gains and dividends.

Then, on top of that, this agreement includes a horrendous proposal regarding the estate tax. The estate tax was enacted in 1916, and it was a proposal strongly supported by Teddy Roosevelt, who believed very strongly that it was not healthy for America to have an ongoing and evolving concentration of ownership. Here is what Teddy Roosevelt said in 1910:

"The absence of effective state, and, especially, national, restraint upon unfair money-getting has tended to create a small class of enormously wealthy and economically powerful men, whose chief object is to hold and increase their power. The prime need is to change the conditions which enable these men to accumulate power which is not for the general welfare that they should hold or exercise. . . . No man should receive a dollar unless that dollar has been fairly earned. Every dollar received should represent a dollar's worth of service rendered—not gambling in stocks, but service rendered. The really big fortune, the swollen fortune, by the mere fact of its size acquires qualities which differentiate it in kind as well as in degree from what is passed by men of relatively small means. Therefore, I believe in a graduated income tax on big fortunes, and in another tax which is far more easily collected and far more effective—a graduated inheritance tax on big fortunes, properly safeguarded against evasion and increasing rapidly in amount with the size of the estate."

How is that? One hundred years ago. That is what he said. I would say he got it right when he said that. It is even more true today, hence the estate tax.

Unfortunately, under the agreement reached by the President and the Republicans, the estate tax rate, which was 55 percent under President Clinton with a $1 million tax exemption when the economy, by the way, was a heck of a lot stronger than it is today, will decline to 35 percent with an exemption on the first $5 million of an individual's estate and $10 million for a couple.

I made this point earlier, but I think it has got to be made over and over. Our Republican friends have renamed the estate tax the death tax. The implication of what they are saying, and what many Americans believe, is that if I have $100,000 in the bank or $50,000 in the bank and I die, my kids are going to have to pay a heavy estate tax on what I left them. But that is absolutely and categorically not the case. The estate tax applies only to the top three-tenths of 1 percent. This is not a tax on the rich. This is a tax on the very, very, very rich. And under this proposal, which benefits only the top three-tenths of 1 percent, the President and the Republicans agreed to lower the tax rate on the estate tax to 35 percent, with an exemption on the first $5 million.

That is wrong. Let me give you an example of who the folks are who will benefit from doing this. Many of my Republican colleagues have been pushing very hard, not just to lower the tax rate—by the way, this 35 percent is lower, I think, than they ever dreamed they would get, with a $5 million exemption, but what they wanted ultimately, and I suspect will continue to fight for, is the complete repeal of the estate tax.

To give one example—and I don't mean to pick on the Walton family, but just as a flesh-and-blood example—Sam Walton's family, the heirs to the Walmart fortune, are worth, give or take, $89 billion. That is a lot of money. The Walton family would receive an estimated $32.7 billion tax break if the estate tax was completely repealed. Does anybody in their right mind believe that when this country has a national debt of $13.8 trillion and when we have the highest rate of childhood poverty in the industrialized world and our unemployment rate is 9.8 percent, can anybody for one second fathom Members of the Senate saying they want to give a $32 billion tax break to one family?

In terms of the estate tax, what we have done is made it even more regressive. We have given substantial help to exactly the people who need it the least. That is not what we should be doing. Our job—and I know it is a radical idea—should be to represent the vast majority of the people, the middle class, the working families, and not just the top 1 or 2 percent. This proposal, this lowering of the estate tax, which will cost our government substantial sums of money because the revenue is not going to come in, will benefit only the top three-tenths of 1 percent.

Again, if some of my Republican colleagues are successful in their desire—and they are moving down the path—if we repeal the estate tax entirely, which is what they want to do—it is hard to believe, and some of the listeners out there think I am kidding, but I am deadly serious—it will drive up the national debt by some $1 trillion over a 10-year period. Lowering the estate tax rate and raising the exemption is clearly an onerous provision.

It is not only the Walton family of Walmart who will benefit. According to Forbes magazine, there are 403 billionaires living in this country with a combined net worth of $1.3 trillion.

That is not shabby. That is pretty good. Anyone lucky enough to inherit this extraordinary wealth would benefit the most from repealing the estate tax.

As Robert Frank wrote in his book *Richistan*: "The wealthiest people in this country accumulated so much wealth that they have been competing to see who could own the largest private yacht, who could own the most private jets, who could own the most expensive cars, jewelry, artwork, et cetera. In 1997, for example, Leslie Wexner, chairman of Limited Brands, the company that owns Victoria's Secret—"

And none of us know what Victoria's Secret is—

"paid a German shipmaker to build what was then the largest private yacht in the United States. It is called *The Limitless*."

Here is a photo. It is a nice boat. It stretches 315 feet and has 3,000 square feet of teakwood and a gym.

According to *Forbes* magazine, Mr. Wexner is one of the wealthiest 400 people in this country, worth an estimated $2.3 billion. Permanently repealing the estate tax would allow Mr. Wexner's two children to inherit all of his wealth without paying a nickel to help this country deal with the enormous problems we have.

I wish Mr. Wexner—I don't know him; I hope he is alive and well—a long life. But I believe strongly that in this country, if we are going to see the middle class survive and our kids do well, we cannot repeal the estate tax and we cannot lower estate tax rates.

I wish to address another issue which I talked about earlier. I think there is some misunderstanding. The Presiding Officer raised this issue at a recent meeting we had. All over the country, people say: Isn't it great that we are going to lower the payroll tax on workers? We are going to go from 6.2 percent, which workers now pay, down to 4.2 percent. People are going to have more money in their pocket, which certainly is a good thing. It is going to cost $120 billion in Social Security payroll taxes.

Here is the point. Yes, we do want to put more money in workers' pockets. That is why many of us in the stimulus package supported a $400-a-year tax break for virtually every worker in America. That is what we said. We want people in these difficult times to have the money to take care of their families. When they have that money, they go out and spend it. When they spend it, it creates other jobs because people have to provide goods and services for them. It has a good, stimulative impact. We do want workers to have more money in their pockets.

While this idea of lowering the payroll tax sounds like a good idea, in truth, it really is not a good idea. This idea originated from very conservative Republicans whose intention from the beginning was to destroy Social Security by choking off the funds that go to it. This is not just Bernie Sanders' analysis. There was recently—I distributed it recently at a meeting we held—a news release that came from the National Committee to Preserve Social Security and Medicare.

The headline on that press release is "Cutting Contributions to Social Security Signals the Beginning of the End. Payroll Tax Holiday is Anything But." What the National Committee to Preserve Social Security and Medicare, which is one of the largest senior groups in America, well understands is that there are people out there who want to destroy Social Security. And one way to do that is to divert funds from the Social Security trust fund.

What the President and others have said is not to worry, this is just a one-year program—just one year. In fact, they say, the General Treasury will pay the difference. So the Social Security trust fund is not going to lose funding.

The reason we have a $2.6 trillion surplus today in Social Security and the reason Social Security is good for the next 27 years to pay out all benefits is because it comes from the payroll tax. It is not dependent upon the whims of the Congress and the Treasury.

The President and Republicans said: This is just a one-year program. Don't worry.

I do worry. I worry that once we establish this one-year payroll tax holiday, next year our Republican friends will say: Do you want to end that? You are going to be raising taxes on workers. And enough people will support that concept, and this one-year payroll tax holiday will become permanent. And when we do that, we will be choking off, over a period of years, trillions of dollars that we need to make sure Social Security is viable and is there for our children and grandchildren.

But don't listen to me. Listen to somebody who knows a lot more about this issue than I do. Barbara Kennelly is a former Congresswoman from Connecticut. She is the president and CEO of the National Committee to Preserve Social Security and Medicare. This is what Barbara Kennelly says:

"Even though Social Security contributed nothing to the current economic crisis, it has been bartered in a deal that provides deficit busting tax cuts for the wealthy. Diverting $120 billion in Social Security contributions for a so-called tax holiday may sound like a good deal for workers now, but it is bad business for a program that a majority of middle class seniors will rely upon in the future."

The headline is "Cutting Contributions to Social Security Signals the Beginning of the End."

This is not a good approach. Providing and figuring out a way that we can get more money into the hands of working people, as we did in the stimulus package, does make a lot of sense. Going forward with a payroll tax holiday is a backdoor method to end up breaking Social Security. It is not anything we should support.

Let me mention a quote from a gentleman who understands this issue very well. He understands the politics of what is going on here. His name Bruce Bartlett, former adviser for Presidents Reagan and George H.W. Bush. He recently wrote the following in opposition to this payroll tax cut. This is what Mr. Bartlett wrote:

"What are the odds that Republicans will ever allow this one-year tax holiday to expire? They wrote the Bush tax cuts with explicit expiration dates and then when it came time for the law they wrote to take effect exactly as they wrote it, they said any failure to extend them permanently would constitute the biggest tax increase in history. . . . if allowing the Bush tax cuts to expire is the biggest tax increase in history, one that Republicans claim would decimate a still-fragile economy, then surely expiration of a payroll tax holiday would also constitute a massive tax increase on the working people of America. . . . Republicans would prefer to destroy Social Security's finances or permanently fund it with general revenues"—switch the revenue base from the payroll tax to general revenues—"than allow a once-suspended payroll tax to be reimposed. Arch Social Security hater Peter Ferrara once told me that funding it with general revenues was part of his plan to destroy it by converting Social Security into a welfare program, rather than an earned benefit. He was right."

In other words, what this issue is about is breaking the bonds we have had since the inception of Social Security where Social Security was paid for by workers. You pay for it when you are working, and you get the benefits when you are old. That is the deal. There is no Federal money coming in from the General Treasury.

This gentleman, Mr. Bartlett, former adviser to Presidents Reagan and George H.W. Bush, thinks—and I suspect he is quite right—this is the beginning of an effort to destroy Social Security.

The real debate about Social Security is not one about finances.

There has been a lot of misinformation and disinformation out there. I hear from some of my friends on the Republican side that Social Security is going bankrupt; it is not going to be there for our kids. That is absolutely not true. Social Security today has a $2.6 trillion surplus. Social Security can pay out every benefit owed to every eligible American, if we do not start diverting funds, for the next 27 years, at which point it pays out about 78 percent of benefits. So our challenge in 27 years is to fill that 22 percent gap. That it is. Can we do it? Sure we can.

President Obama, when he was campaigning, and I think he has repeated since, made the very good suggestion that instead of having a cap in terms of which people contribute into the fund at $106,800, what we should do is do a bubble, and income of $250,000 or more should not be exempt from the Social Security Payroll Tax. If you did that and nothing else, you have essentially solved the Social Security problem for the next 75 years. Very easy. It is done.

So what this payroll tax holiday is doing, in my view, is pretty dangerous. I do not think enough people understand that. I think that is one of the strong reasons this agreement should be opposed.

Another reason I believe this agreement is not as good an agreement as we can get is that it provides tens and tens of billions of dollars in tax cuts for various types of businesses. I am not here to say these tax cuts cannot do some good. I suspect they can. But I think there is a lot better way to create the jobs we need than providing these particular business tax cuts.

Frankly, I think economists from almost all political spectrums—conservative to progressive—understand that if we are serious about creating the kinds of jobs this economy desperately needs and if we want to do that as rapidly and as cost-effectively as we possibly can, the way to do that is not to provide business tax cuts because right now—right now—corporate America is sitting on close to $2 trillion cash on hand. They have a ton of money. The problem is the products they are creating are not being bought by the American people because the American people do not have the money to buy those goods and services.

So if we are serious about creating the jobs we need, I think what we have to do is start making significant investments in our crumbling infrastructure; that is, rebuilding our bridges, our roads, our water systems, broadband, cell phone service, public transportation, our rail system, dams. In every single one of these areas, we are seeing our infrastructure crumbling.

The point is, if you simply ignore a crumbling infrastructure—and I say this as a former mayor who dealt with this issue—if you simply ignore a crumbling infrastructure, do you know what, it does not get better all by itself.

I know many mayors and Governors would very much like to think they could turn their backs on the infrastructure because it is not a sexy investment. It is not a sexy investment. But the reality is, if you do not pay attention to it today, it only gets worse and it costs you more money. It is like having a cavity. You can get your cavity filled. If you neglect it, as I have, and you end up doing a root canal, it is far more painful, far more expensive. That is what it is about. Do we maintain our infrastructure? Clearly, we have not. According to the American Society of Civil Engineers, we should be spending about $2.2 trillion in the next five years in order to maintain our infrastructure.

I say to the Presiding Officer, I do not know about Alaska—I spent a very brief time in the Presiding Officer's beautiful state—but I do know in Vermont we have bridges all over our state that are in desperate need of repair. It is fair to say that the stimulus package has been very positive for my state. We are spending more money on roads and bridges. But we have a long way to go. So we are putting money into our roads and bridges. We are hiring people to do that work. That is what we should be doing all over the country.

But it is not just roads and bridges. It is water systems. I told this story, I guess a few hours ago now, about a mayor, the mayor of Rutland, Vermont, which is the second largest city in the state. I was in his office and he showed me a pipe, and the pipe was in pretty bad shape. He said: You know, this pipe was laid by an engineer who then, after he did this, went off to war. And he said: What war do you think he went off to fight? And he said it was the Civil War—the Civil War. So this was pipe laid in Rutland, Vermont, which is still being used, which was laid, I am guessing, in the 1850s, maybe 1860s. And it is not just Rutland, Vermont.

When I was mayor of Burlington, we had to spend $50 million, back then, 20 years ago, I think, rebuilding our wastewater plants and making sure that a lot of pollution and filthy water did not get into our beautiful lake, Lake Champlain. It was an expensive proposition. But right now, we are going to have to invest in that. It is our water systems, our dams, our levees, our roads, our bridges.

I mentioned earlier and contrasted what was going on in infrastructure in the United States as opposed to China, and I quoted from a book called *Third World America*, written by Arianna Huffington, who tells us, essentially, if we do not get our act together, that is what we will become—a Third World country.

She points out that compared to countries such as China, our investments in rail are absolutely pathetic and inadequate. In China, right now, that country is investing billions and billions of dollars in high-speed rail, building thousands and thousands of miles of high-speed rail. They are building about 100 new airports. And what are we doing?

So one of my many objections to the proposal struck between the President and the Republican leadership is I think we can do better in job creation than in business tax cuts. There is a time and a place for business tax cuts, and I am not against them. But I would say that at this particular moment in American history, at this particular moment, it makes a lot more sense to create, over a period of years, millions of jobs rebuilding our rail system, our subways, our roads, our bridges, and our water systems, and many other aspects of our infrastructure.

There are places in Vermont and throughout this country where people cannot today get decent-quality broadband service, cannot get cell phone service. In that area, we are behind many other countries around the world. When we make those investments in infrastructure, we not only create jobs, but we make our country stronger and more productive, and we enable ourselves to compete effectively in the international economy.

Another one of my objections to this proposal and why I think we can do a lot better is that I was really quite disturbed to hear the President and others, who defend this proposal, talk about that one of the "compromises" that was struck was to extend unemployment benefits for 13 months.

To my mind, as I have said earlier, at a time of deep recession, at a time of terribly high unemployment, it would be absolutely wrong and immoral for us to turn our backs on the millions of workers who are about to lose their unemployment benefits. If we do that, it is hard to imagine what happens to those families, for many of whom this is their only source of income. What do they do? Do they lose their homes? Do they move out onto the streets? How do they take care of their kids? I do not know. There are parts of this country where it is very hard to get a job. Long-term unemployment is at the highest level I think we have ever seen in recorded history. You cannot turn your backs on those families.

But I get upset when I hear that the Republican's willingness to support an extension of unemployment benefits for 13 months is a major compromise. I will tell you—I think a lot of the American people do not know this—that for the past 40 years—40 years, four decades—under both Democratic and Republican administrations, whenever the unemployment rate has been above 7.2 percent—and today we are at 9.8 percent unemployment—always, whether the Democrats were in control, the Republicans were in control, the President was Democrat, the President was Republican, what people did was say: We have to extend unemployment benefits. It is kind of common sense. It is not partisan. So when you have a program that has existed for 40 years in a bipartisan effort, it sounds to me that it is not much of a compromise for the Republicans to say: OK, we will do what Democrats and Republicans have done for 40 years. What a major compromise. It is not a compromise. It is just continuing existing bipartisan policy, which is sensible. It is sensible from a moral perspective. You cannot leave fellow American families out high and dry.

It is good economics because what the economists tell us is the people who will spend that money quickest are people who receive unemployment compensation because that is all they have. They are going to go out and buy, and when they buy from the neighborhood store, they create jobs. So it is good economics, and it is the moral thing to do.

But, frankly, in my view, this is not much of a compromise. This is just continuing four decades of existing policies.

As I said earlier, there are very clearly positive parts of this agreement, no question about it. I think almost every American will tell you that it would be totally absurd—I know there are some who disagree, but I think the vast majority of Americans believe that in a time when the middle class is collapsing, when median family income has gone down, when unemployment is high, that it would be a real horror show if we did not extend the Bush tax breaks for the middle class, for 98 percent of American workers—98 percent. That is what we want.

We could have crafted it much tighter, couldn't we have? We could have said: Nobody above $100,000, nobody above $150,000. That is pretty generous. We said a family earning up to $250,000 should get an extension of these tax breaks. That is 98 percent of the American people, and that is not good enough for our Republican friends. They are fighting tooth and nail to make sure the top 2 percent—the millionaires and billionaires, the CEOs who earn tens of millions a year—they are fighting—it is as if they are at war. They are so engaged to make sure these fabulously wealthy people receive at least $1 million, in some cases. For people who are making $1 million a year, they are going to receive, on average, $100,000 a year in tax breaks. For the very, very wealthiest, it could be over $1 million a year.

I say to the Presiding Officer, I know you joined me just two days ago in saying that at a time when senior citizens in this country and disabled vets, for two years in a row, had not received any COLA, that maybe it was the right thing to do—because we know that health care costs and prescription drug costs are soaring—that maybe we should provide a $250 check for those seniors and disabled veterans one time—one time. I could not get one Republican vote in support of that proposition. We won 53 to 45, but around here it does not take 50 votes to win; it does not take a majority to win; it takes 60 votes. We could not get one Republican vote. So here you have every Republican voting against a $250 check for a disabled vet or a senior citizen who is living on $15,000, $16,000 a year. Cannot afford it. But we can afford a million-dollar-a-year tax break for somebody who is worth hundreds of millions of dollars.

Now, somebody may understand that rationale. I don't. I really don't. I can't understand it. I can't understand asking our kids and grandchildren to pay more in taxes, and the national debt goes up in order to provide tax breaks for the richest people in this country.

So while there are some good provisions in this bill—certainly extending the tax breaks for 98 percent of our working people, for the very broad middle class. I think if the American people demand it, in our democracy we can do better. I don't know if the Presiding Officer or I alone will be able to convince some of our Republican friends or maybe some of our Democratic friends to make this into the kind of proposal we need for the working families of this country, and for our children, for our next generation. I don't know if we can do it inside this Beltway.

As I said earlier, I think the way we win this battle, the way we defeat this proposal and come back with a much better proposal is when millions of Americans start writing and e-mailing and calling their Senators, their Congress people, and say: Wait a second. Are you nuts? Do you really think millionaires and billionaires need a huge tax break at a time when this country has a $13.8 trillion national debt? What are you smoking? How could you for one second think that makes any sense whatsoever?

I will tell the Presiding Officer something. I don't know what my phones are doing today in my office right now. But in the last three days we have gotten, I am guessing, 5,000 phone calls and e-mails, and about 99 percent of them are in disagreement with this proposal.

I am looking at a chart. We have gotten 2,100 calls that just came in today. I don't know what kind of calls other Members of the Senate are getting, but certainly those are the calls I am getting.

This point cannot be made strongly enough: What our Republican friends want to do—and they have been pretty honest and up front about it, especially some of the extreme, right-wing people who have been running for office and, in some cases, have won—they have been honest enough to say they want to bring this country back to where we were in the 1920s. Their ultimate aim is the basic repeal of almost all of the provisions that have been passed in the last 70 years to protect working people, the elderly, and children. They believe in a Darwinian-style society in which you have the survival of the fittest; that we are not a society which comes together to take care of all of us. You take care of me in need and I take care of you and your family; that we are one people. Their strategy is pretty clear. They want to ultimately destroy Social Security.

What we are beginning to hear more and more of is why don't we raise the retirement age to 68 or 69. That deficit reduction commission, which I thought was—the people on that commission were bad appointees by the President. We could have put together some good economists to say how do we in a fair way—in a fair way—address the deficit and national debt crisis. That wasn't what that commission did. So these folks are talking about major cuts in Social Security, Medicare, Medicaid.

At a time when it is so hard for young people to afford to go to college, they want to raise the costs by asking our young people while they are in college to be accruing interest on their loans.

So I think if the President believes that if this agreement is passed, the Republicans are going to come to the table and we are all going to live happily in the future, we are all going to work together in a nonpartisan way, I think he is not understanding the reality. These people are going to come back and they are going to come back very aggressively for major cuts in Social Security, Medicare, Medicaid, environmental protection, education, childcare, Pell grants, you name it, because their belief is—I don't quite understand it—that it is somehow good public policy to give tax breaks for the wealthiest people in this country who, in many ways, have never had it so good, while you cut programs that the middle class and working families of this country desperately depend upon.

So I would suggest that this big debate we are having right now on whether we should accept the proposal agreed to by the President and the Republicans is just the beginning of what is coming down the pike. If we surrender now on this issue, we can expect next month and the following month another governmental crisis, another threat of a shutdown, unless they get their way. So I think rather than asking the working families of this country to have to compromise, instead of asking our kids to pay more in taxes to bail out billionaires, maybe—I know this is a radical idea—but maybe we should ask a handful of our Republican friends to join us. Maybe a handful of honest conservatives over there who have been telling us for years their great concerns about deficit spending and a huge national debt, maybe they should be prepared to vote against the proposal which raises the national debt and our deficit by giving tax breaks to some of the richest people in the world.

Quite frankly, I don't think I am going to be able to convince them. I don't know that the Presiding Officer is going to be able to convince them. But I think their constituents can convince them. I think the American people can convince them. I think, as I said earlier, if the American people stand up, we can defeat this proposal and we can create a much better proposal.

Clearly, we must extend tax breaks for the middle class. Clearly, we must make sure unemployed workers continue to get the benefits they desperately need. But equally, clearly, we must make sure we are not raising the national debt which, as sure as I am standing here, will result in cuts in Social Security and Medicare and Medicaid and education and other programs if this proposal is passed.

So this is not only an important proposal unto itself: $900 billion plus even in Washington is nothing to sneeze at. But it is an important proposal in terms of the direction in which our country goes into the future. If we accept this proposal of a two-year extension for the richest people in America, I believe it will eventually become either a long-term extension or a permanent extension. If we accept the proposal that lowers the rates on the estate tax which benefits only the top three-tenths of 1 percent—99.7 percent of Americans get nothing—but if we give them what they want, I believe over a period of years it will lead to the complete abolishment and ending of the estate tax which will cost us about $1 trillion over a 10-year period.

So I hope this issue is not one just progressives or moderates feel strongly about. I hope honest conservatives, who in their heart of hearts believe this country is seriously in danger when we have unsustainable deficits and a huge national debt, will tell their elected officials here in Washington not to pass a piece of legislation which increases the national debt significantly and, in fact, will allow for the permanent—over years, in my view—extension of these tax breaks.

So that is what this debate is about. It is about fundamentally whether we continue the process by which the richest people in this country become richer, at a time when we have the most unequal distribution of income and wealth of any major country on Earth.

As I have said earlier, this is not an issue that is discussed—I don't know—well, I do know why. It is just not an issue that people feel comfortable talking about because they don't want to offend their wealthy campaign contributors or take on the lobbyists who are out there. But that is the reality. Throughout the entire world, the United States has the most unequal distribution of income. The top 1 percent is earning 23.5 percent of all income. That is more than the bottom 50 percent. That is not just immoral, it is bad economics because if the middle class gets crushed entirely, who is going to be buying the goods and services produced in this economy?

So this piece of legislation, as important as it is unto itself—and it is very important—is equally important in terms of what it says about where we are going into the future. Are we going to protect the middle class and working families of our country? Are we going to make sure every young person in America, regardless of income, has the ability to go to college, or are we going to allow college to become unaffordable for hundreds and hundreds of thousands of bright, young people, or else force them to leave school deeply in debt?

Are we going to create a health care system which guarantees health care to all of our people—high-quality health care—or are we going to continue a situation where 45,000 Americans die each year because they don't have access to a doctor? Are we going to invest in our energy system so we break our dependence on foreign oil? We spend about $350 billion a year importing oil from Saudi Arabia and other foreign countries—almost $1 billion a day—which should be used to make this country energy independent, which should be used to transform our energy system away from fossil fuel into energy efficiency and sustainable energy, technologies such as wind, solar, geothermal, and biomass.

By the way, none of that has been addressed, as I understand it, in this proposal.

So my point is not just that this proposal is a bad proposal as it stands before us now, but it is going to move us in the future in a direction that I do not believe this country should be going.

I mentioned earlier my own personal family's history is the history of millions and millions of Americans. My father, as it happened, came to this country at the age of 17 without a nickel in his pocket. He worked hard his whole life. He never made very much money, but he and my mom—my mom graduated high school; she never went to college—had the satisfaction, the very significant satisfaction, of knowing their kids got a college education. My older brother Larry went to law school, and I graduated from the University of Chicago.

I think what is going on in this country and why the anxiety level is so high is not just that people are worried about themselves—parents worry more about their kids than they do about themselves. But what parents are sitting around and worrying about now is they are saying: Will, for the first time in the modern history of this country, my kids have a lower standard of living than their parents?

Will my kids earn less income? Will my kids not have the education I have? Will my kids not have the opportunity to travel and learn and grow as I have done? Are the best days of

America behind us? That is really the question. I don't think that has to be the case.

But I will tell my colleagues, as I mentioned earlier, if we are going to change the national priorities in this country, if we are going to start devoting our energy and our attention to the needs of working families and the middle class, we have to defeat this proposal and we have to defeat similar types of proposals which come down the pike. When this country has a $13.8 trillion national debt, it is insane—nothing less than insane—to be talking about huge tax breaks for people who don't need them. Again, as I mentioned earlier, ironically, we have a lot of these millionaires out there who apparently love their country more than some of the people in this Chamber.

You have some of the richest people in America—Bill Gates and all the good, charitable work he does, and Warren Buffet and many others—who are saying: I am doing just fine. I am a billionaire or a multimillionaire. I don't need your tax breaks. I am worried about the fact that we have the highest rate of childhood poverty: invest in our children. I am worried that our infrastructure is crumbling: invest in our infrastructure. I am worried that 45,000 Americans are dying this year who don't have access to health care: invest in health care. I am worried about global warming: invest in transforming our energy system. These are patriotic Americans. They love their country. They are saying to us: We don't even want it.

So we are giving money to people who, in some cases, don't even want it. I do know there are others out there who do want it. I think if there is one issue that we as a Congress and a government have to address, it is the extraordinary level of greed in this country. We have to stand tall and draw a line in the sand and simply say: Enough is enough. How much do you want? How much do you need? How many yachts can you own? How many homes can you have? Isn't it enough that the top 1 percent now earns 23.5 percent of the income in this country? How much more do they want? Do they want 30 percent, 35 percent? Isn't it enough that the top 1 percent owns more wealth than the bottom 90 percent? How much more do they need?

I mentioned earlier, when I talked about the situation that got us into this horrendous recession—and that is the collapse of Wall Street—I talked about what I think most Americans understand very well; that is, the incredible greed and recklessness and dishonesty that exists on Wall Street. We must not allow ourselves to encourage and continue the kind of greed we have seen in recent years. It is an abomination that the people who caused this economic crisis—the worst recession since the Great Depression—that the people on Wall Street who caused it are now earning more money than they did before we bailed them out.

Earlier today, I was reading some e-mails that came to my office from Vermonters who were struggling to keep their heads above water. They were terribly painful and poignant stories about honest, good, decent people who are now choosing whether they should put gas in their car or buy the food or prescription drugs they need. It is not just a Vermont story; it is an American story. It is a reality out there for tens of millions of Americans.

In my view, we can negotiate a much better agreement than the one President Obama and the Republican leadership did. There are some good parts of that agreement, which obviously should be retained and perhaps even strengthened. Those include, of course, making sure we extend unemployment benefits to those who need it and, of course, that we extend tax breaks for the middle class. There are some other very good provisions in there which I think are worthwhile.

I think if the American people stand and agree with those of us who say no more tax breaks for the very wealthiest people in this country, we can defeat this proposal, and we can come up with a much better one that is fairer to the middle class of this country and is fairer to our young children.

I do not want to see our young kids—my children and grandchildren—have a lower standard of living than their parents. That is not what America is about. What I think we have to do is defeat this proposal. I think we have to urge our fellow Americans to stand and say no to tax breaks for those who don't need it. I think we have to work in a very serious way about creating the millions and millions of good-paying jobs that this country desperately needs. I personally believe that is a far more effective approach than giving the variety of business taxes that were in this proposal at a time when corporate America is sitting on $2 million of unused cash. They have the money. I think a much better approach, as I said earlier, is investing in our crumbling infrastructure. I think that makes us healthier and stronger as a nation for the future and in the global economy.

I think it creates jobs quicker and in a more cost-effective way than these tax cuts. I also think it is high time the American people move—they want us to move in an entirely new direction in terms of trade. I am always amazed how Republicans and Democrats alike—and I speak as the longest serving Independent in Congress—come election time, have ads on television saying: Oh, we have to do something about outsourcing and about our trade policy. But somehow, the day after the election, when corporate America continues to throw American workers out on the street and moves to China, moves to other low-wage countries, that discussion ceases to exist and that legislation never seems to appear.

So it seems to me we have to defeat this proposal, and that in defeating this, we are going to tell the American people there are at least some of us here who understand what our jobs and obligations are: that is, that we are supposed to represent them, the middle class of the country, and not just wealthy campaign contributors or bow to the interests of the lobbyists who are all over this place.

When I talked a moment ago about the need to invest in our infrastructure as a way to create jobs, being more cost-effective than some of these business tax breaks, I am looking now at a *Wall Street Journal* article of December 9, 2010. Here is the headline: "Companies Clinging to Cash; Coffers Swell to 51-year High as Cautious Firms Put Off Investing in Growth."

That is a story by Justin Lahart. Here is the story. It makes the point I have been trying to express:

"Corporate America's cash pile has hit its highest level in half a century. Rather than pouring their money into building plants or hiring workers, nonfinancial companies in the United States are sitting on $1.93 trillion in cash"

—I said $2 trillion, but it is $1.93 trillion in cash—

"and other liquid assets at the end of September, up from $1.8 trillion at the end of June, the Federal Reserve said Thursday. Cash accounted for 7.4 percent of the companies' total assets, the largest share since 1959. The cash buildup shows the deep caution many companies feel about investing in expansion, while the economic recovery remains painfully slow, and high unemployment and battered household finances continue to limit consumers' ability to spend."

What have we been talking about? The *Wall Street Journal* is not my favorite paper, but they are saying that the way you are going to get the economy moving again is to put money in the hands of working people, who will then go out and buy the goods and services these companies produce. I have my doubts about whether these tax cuts will, in fact, have the desired result.

As I said earlier, and will say again, I think the most effective way to create jobs, and the most important way, is to rebuild our crumbling infrastructure. That is our roads, bridges, rail system, water system, wastewater plants, our dams, levees, and the need to improve broadband to make sure every community in America has access to good-quality broadband and access to cell phone service. Unfortunately, as best as I can understand, there has not been one nickel appropriated in this proposed legislation that would go to infrastructure improvements.

I think this proposal should be defeated because it is not a strong proposal for the middle class. It is a proposal that gives much too much to people who don't need it, and it is a proposal that I think sets the stage for similar-type proposals down the pike. I apologize to anybody who has been listening for any length of time. I know I have been, to say the least, a bit repetitious.

But the concern is that when the President and some of my Republican colleagues talk about some of these tax breaks being temporary, we are just going to extend them for two years, talking about this payroll tax holiday being just one year, I have been in Washington long enough to know that assertion doesn't fly; that what is temporary today is long-term tomorrow and is permanent the next day. I fear very much that this proposal is bad on the surface. I fear very much that this proposal will lead us down a very bad track in terms of more trickle-down economics, which benefits the tricklers and not the ordinary Americans. I think it is a proposal that should be defeated.

The point I wish to make is not just my point of view. I think it should be defeated. I think we can do a lot better. I have to tell you the calls that are coming into my office are—here is what we got today: 2,122 calls oppose the deal, and I think 100 calls are supportive of the deal. You can do the arithmetic on it. At least 95 percent of the calls I got to-day are saying this is not a good deal. We can do better.

I know that in the last three or four days we have gotten probably 6,000 or 7,000 calls that say this. This is not just Vermont—many of those calls come from out of state, by the way. But I think that is true all over this country.

Let me conclude. It has been a long day. Let me simply say I believe the proposal that was developed by the President and the Republicans is nowhere near as good as we can achieve. I don't know that we are able ourselves to get the handful of Republicans we need to say no to this agreement. I do believe that if the American people stand—by the way, it may not just be Republicans. There may be some Democrats as well. If the American people stand and say: We can do better than this; we don't need to drive up the national debt by giving tax breaks to millionaires and billionaires, that if the American people are prepared to stand and we are prepared to follow them, I think we can defeat this proposal and come up with a better proposal which reflects the needs of working-class and middle-class families of our country and, to me, most importantly, the children of our country.

With that, I yield the floor and I suggest the absence of a quorum.

Index

SENATOR BERNIE SANDERS is the longest-serving independent in the history of the US Congress. He has represented Vermont in the Senate for two terms and in the House for sixteen years. He also served four terms as mayor of Burlington, Vermont. In 2015, he announced his candidacy for president of the United States.

The Nation Institute

NATION BOOKS

Founded in 2000, **Nation Books** has become a leading voice in American independent publishing. The inspiration for the imprint came from the *Nation* magazine, the oldest independent and continuously published weekly magazine of politics and culture in the United States.

The imprint's mission is to produce authoritative books that break new ground and shed light on current social and political issues. We publish established authors who are leaders in their area of expertise, and endeavor to cultivate a new generation of emerging and talented writers. With each of our books we aim to positively affect cultural and political discourse.

Nation Books is a project of The Nation Institute, a nonprofit media center dedicated to strengthening the independent press and advancing social justice and civil rights. The Nation Institute is home to a dynamic range of programs: the award-winning Investigative Fund, which supports ground-breaking investigative journalism; the widely read and syndicated website TomDispatch; the Victor S. Navasky Internship Program in conjunction with the *Nation* magazine; and Journalism Fellowships that support up to 25 high-profile reporters every year.

For more information on Nation Books, The Nation Institute, and the *Nation* magazine, please visit:

www.nationbooks.org

www.nationinstitute.org

www.thenation.com

www.facebook.com/nationbooks.ny

Twitter: @nationbooks